D0374553

FINDING
THE
UNCOMMON
DEAL

FINDING THE UNCOMMON DEAL

A Top New York Lawyer Explains How to
Buy a Home For the Lowest Possible Price

ADAM LEITMAN BAILEY

WILEY

John Wiley & Sons, Inc.

Published by John Wiley & Sons, Inc., Hoboken, New Jersey.
Published simultaneously in Canada.

For general information on our other products and services or for technical support, please contact our Customer Care Department within the United States at (800) 762-2974, outside the United States at (317) 572-3993 or fax (317) 572-4002.

Wiley also publishes its books in a variety of electronic formats. Some content that appears in print may not be available in electronic books. For more information about Wiley products, visit our web site at www.wiley.com.

Library of Congress Cataloging-in-Publication Data:

Bailey, Adam Leitman.
    Finding the uncommon deal: a top New York lawyer explains how to buy a home for the lowest possible price/Adam Leitman Bailey.
        p.   cm.
    Includes index.
    ISBN 978-0-470-94366-3 (pbk.)
    ISBN 978-1-118-02802-5 (ebk)
    ISBN 978-1-118-02803-2 (ebk)
    ISBN 978-1-118-02804-9 (ebk)
        1. House buying.   2. Residential real estate–Purchasing.   3. Housing–Prices.
I. Title.
    HD1375.B225 2011
    643'.12–dc22

                                                                    2010045240

Printed in the United States of America

10 9 8 7 6 5 4 3 2 1

To everyone who grew up (like me) without business-savvy parents to teach them the lessons in this book.

Contents

Foreword

I had been living in a rental apartment on 34th Street in New York for over a year when my landlord mentioned she was interested in selling and asked if I would be interested in buying. I loved my apartment, so I knew this was a great opportunity for me to step into the realm of ownership, while reducing my monthly costs at the same time. I was 32 years old, had never owned property before, and as excited as I was about the prospect, I was terrified about it too. That was when a dear friend of mine mentioned Adam Bailey's name as that of an attorney I should speak to about the deal. Best move I ever made!

Now in hindsight, it was a rather simple deal; although it's fair to say that your average transaction outside New York City could never compare to the complications involved with buying a NYC co-op. This was also a period of time when banks made things extremely easy on the lender—something we may never see again—in my lifetime anyway. But what I got from Adam then, and what I continue to receive a decade later, is a boiled-down, layman's education in how it all works.

Adam is a natural-born teacher, and he genuinely thrives on helping people do what he sincerely and passionately loves doing himself: buying real estate—a passion that I joke with him about as being evident in the speed with which he talks. If you ever have the privilege of hearing him speak, you'll know what I mean when you come away extremely inspired, somewhat exhausted, and very much in love with real estate, whether you planned to be or not. His written word, as you'll find here, has a similar effect—minus the exhaustion.

Flash-forward 10 years, and I am now a real estate investor with properties in upstate New York, New Orleans, Nashville, and yes, I still have that little co-op on 34th Street. I'd like to think that I'm one of the clients Adam refers to as an inspiration for writing this book. In fact, the chapters of *Finding the Uncommon Deal* eerily read like answers to the various, and seemingly random, questions I've peppered him with over the years. As it turns out, there was nothing random about my questions after all. It's just that the intricacies of any one real estate purchase can be so extremely vast that the parts don't always seem to connect at first. Furthermore, most buyers never have the same experience as their friends, families, or neighbors, and no one property buying experience is ever the same as the last one.

One thing that I believe this book does exceptionally well is to paint a picture of the real estate purchasing puzzle in a linear fashion so that the pieces always make sense in context, even if you encounter them way out of order as I frequently have. Adam does this by walking you through the steps from the beginning to the middle and all the way through closing a property purchase of any kind.

When I decided to become a professional investor five years ago (a move I felt necessary to offset the inherent instability of a career in entertainment), I began filling my personal library with books that covered the specific areas of real estate I was interested in, and my library as a result is huge, with more than 30 books directly related to buying real estate. While I have found each one invaluable in its own way, what they all add up to as individual resources can be found boiled down in these pages, written in easy to understand terms. The more complicated concepts are illustrated through Adam's real life stories, many of which I can relate to directly myself, and the lessons learned are summarized in easy to reference "Insider Tips" at the end of the chapters.

Is it a one-stop shop for a professional real estate investor? No. It wasn't meant to be. A book of that sort would likely be 10,000 pages long or more. What *Finding the Uncommon Deal* is, however, lies right in the title; it's what you must know before buying a home . . . period.

I highly recommend reading this book at any stage of your real estate experience. Go forth with home buying confidence, knowing you have what I believe to be the most comprehensive home buying resource, written by one of the most respected and knowledgeable real estate attorneys, investors, educators, and mentors in the country.

—Evan Farmer

About Evan Farmer

Evan Farmer was host, carpenter, and handyman of The Learning Channel's Emmy-nominated series, While You Were Out, *and host and designer for HGTV's Freestyle. Evan first reached stardom performing as part of the MTV hit boy band 2GE+HER. He currently owns and co-owns five investment properties in three states and in 2003 he co-founded Renovolution, a company whose mission is to provide affordable housing to struggling families in New Orleans. You can find more information about Evan at www.evanfarmer.net.*

Preface   Greed, Fear, and
Opportunity in the
New Real Estate
Environment

The book is an insider's guide to finding the best home for the cheapest price in the new real estate economy. Incredible deals are on the market ready to be made, but only for those buyers who know how to seize them. By divulging insiders' secrets, legal maneuvers, the tricks of the trade, and many experts' lifelong experiences in scoring deals, my goal is to put you at an uncommon advantage.

USING THIS BOOK TO OBTAIN THE GREATEST HOME AT THE CHEAPEST PRICE

The advice and tactics in this book do not come from being a reporter or doing interviews of other experts for a living. I live and breathe real estate as a real estate lawyer, broker, and home investor. All fluff, page fillers, and unnecessary information have been removed. My life, my businesses, and my legal practice have been dedicated to real estate and attempting to make the United States a better place to live by advocating for smarter real estate decisions. My audacious goal has been to make this the best book on buying a home ever written.

It started when I was unable to find a book on home buying to recommend to my clients and peers. When the economic collapse occurred, I began writing this book to educate buyers and give them an advantage in the dramatically changed real estate environment.

Each paragraph of each chapter of this book gives buyers practical, real life advice and gems that work to protect their planned investments and to help them to understand the process and save money at the same time.

THE BURSTING OF THE NATIONAL REAL ESTATE BUBBLE CREATED INCREDIBLE BUYING OPPORTUNITIES

Before the Great Recession, homeownership allowed owners to garner large profits without having to make any significant investment decisions and with limited risk. As the bubble burst, so did real estate's traditional buying rules. In the aftermath, savvy buyers can now find some of the greatest buying opportunities in the history of real estate.

No real estate market has endured such a game changing disruption of the economy and its real estate rules as we are experiencing today. Shifting lending rules, a record breaking number of persons forced to sell to ward off foreclosure, new private and governmental buying incentives, as well as dozens of new home buying and lending laws, rules, standards and even new vocabulary have scared off many buyers. But educated and aggressive homebuyers have found uncommon deals, and you can too. This book will explain to you the new rules and how to take advantage of them.

FINDING THE UNCOMMON DEAL

Introduction

Should You Buy or Rent?

THE GREATEST PRODUCER OF WEALTH FOR AMERICAN FAMILIES

Real estate is not without challenges. Some deals are better than others, and other deals can be clearly unwise. No deal is worse than one for the home you cannot afford to buy and maintain. Another challenge is that real estate transactions move slowly.

But looking at the last 100 years, real estate has frequently surpassed all other means of garnering wealth, including trading on the stock market. Forbes.com reported a 247 percent increase in home sale prices between 1980 and 2004. The statement attributed to Mark Twain, Will Rogers, and many others, "Buy land—they're not making any more of it," while an undoubted overstatement, holds a significant truth. Everyone needs a place to live. This need for shelter, combined with planet Earth's limited inventory of available homes as a result of the scarcity of land and the ever-growing population, makes real estate an extremely valuable possession, both financially and for the shelter it provides.

Millions of retired homeowners have used their houses as a key part of their financial security. In addition to the peace of mind that comes with not having to pay a mortgage, these homeowners also have the option of cashing in by selling their homes, downsizing, and banking the profits. A home provides shelter as well as financial benefits to its owner in the form of tax deductions and possible appreciation in value.

Basic economic theory talks about the law of supply and demand. And there is one thing you can bank on: The supply of usable land will never keep pace with the demand for it.

Despite the potential for buildings and homes to be built taller and wider, vertically and horizontally, to afford greater capacity, in addition to the ability for new space to be created by expanding landfills into rivers and waters, such methods have been traditionally limited by governments and by natural threats, such as earthquakes. Looking at the history of the United States of America, as the amount of new land fails to keep pace with even a fraction of the growth of the population, the value of real estate has continued to appreciate. Since the end of the Civil War, this country has endured very few periods where the monetary value of the land has not increased during the time an average owner has title to it.

The scarcity of land has resulted in home buying becoming most Americans' greatest financial investment. In the past hundred years, as the majority of economic studies have shown, no other investment has seen the increase in value that property has as a result of land appreciation. Economist Robert J. Schiller charted the sale prices of standard homes for more than a hundred years. Taking inflation into consideration, his findings demonstrated that if a standard home sold in 1890 for $100,000 in today's dollars, a home of the same standard would sell for $199,000 in 2006.

Yet more amazing is that this greatest long-term producer of wealth, comparatively speaking, requires very little maintenance expense, while at the same time it provides for the fundamental life need of shelter.

Long-term homeownership can result in increased wealth for homeowners without having to jump through traditional moneymaking hoops. Homeowners don't have to meet deadlines, sell a product, work overtime, sweat behind a desk, or deal with office politics.

Historically, homeowners have been able to increase wealth simply by owning and maintaining the expenses of a home over a long period of time. Studies have demonstrated that most people have more equity in their homes than in any other asset, including retirement accounts, stocks, and savings accounts.

THE UNITED STATES GOVERNMENT ENCOURAGES HOMEOWNERSHIP

The U.S. government has promoted homeownership through showering homebuyers with tax benefits, credits, and other economic incentives. To this day, no program has awarded renters similar benefits. Homeowners are generally allowed to deduct interest paid on a mortgage and mortgage insurance premiums as well as state and local real estate taxes from their yearly federal and state tax returns. Additionally, homeowners can borrow against their home's equity and receive tax deductions for interest paid. Many government administrations have provided temporary additional tax incentives to encourage home buying, including deductions equaling 10 percent of the purchase price of a home.

THE PRIDE OF HAVING A PLACE TO CALL YOUR OWN

Next to relationships with children and family, homeownership is one of the most satisfying achievements for most people. Much research links homeownership with increased self-esteem and well-being levels. A 1996 study by Balfour and Smith showed that through the purchase of a home a person's status in society is elevated and they feel more of a sense of security and pride. Researchers Rohe and Basolo surveyed homebuyers three years after purchase and found them to have statistically significantly higher life satisfaction levels compared to those still renting properties. In a study by Rossi and Weber, owners repeatedly rated themselves happier than renters did. Trulia's American Dream Survey (2009) revealed that despite the economic downturn, more than three in four Americans still see buying a home as part of the American Dream.

Homeownership is such an important privilege that it is even protected in amendments to the U. S. Constitution. Every homeowner has the security of knowing that no person may enter a law-abiding citizen's home without permission (for renters, landlords usually have the right to enter the premises under certain conditions).

THE TIME TO BUY

For our forebears, the American Dream was not simply getting the home—it was also the hard work, toil, self-restraint, and prudent decision-making that went into making the dream come true. The traditional real estate success story—a home purchase appreciating in value tenfold over the course of a single generation—always entailed three abilities in the purchaser: the ability come up with at least 10 percent of the purchase price at closing; the ability to manage the monthly mortgage payments; and the ability to carry both the mortgage and the necessary maintenance of the home (taxes, repairs, and utilities). Most successful owners spent many years saving as much money as possible in order to garner the entry fee to home buying: the down payment.

All this went out the window during the real estate bubble and subsequent nightmare that our country recently experienced. The United States traded in sound real estate practice for a casino and an automated teller machine. Borrowers purchased homes with mortgages that they simply could never afford. They bet that interest rates would remain low and that property values would always increase. Despite decades where the conventional loan required at least a 10 percent down payment at closings, banks began to finance the entire purchase price and, in some instances, even above it. While borrowers saw this as free money, it was anything but; it was just more unaffordable debt.

The hangover from this real estate boom has led many overextended mortgage borrowers to lose all of their savings, destroy their credit, and have homes taken in foreclosure.

In order to save you that grief, I have prepared an entire chapter in this book to help you determine if you are ready to make the leap to homeownership. If you learn that the cost of owning a home is not something you can currently afford, just keep filling your savings account until you really are ready to make your dream come true. It is far better to wait a few more years to be able to afford a home than to buy a home and lose it, possibly destroying your chances to have some other lender take a chance on you in the future.

THE COST OF BUYING AND MAINTAINING A HOME

The multiple costs involved in the purchase of a home can be grouped into two categories: the costs of taking ownership of a home and the costs of maintaining ownership. Both categories are discussed in detail in later chapters. The costs of taking ownership of a home include the down payment, closing costs, home inspection/engineer's fee, initial payments for homeowner's insurance, and the initial mortgage payment. The yearly costs of maintaining a home generally include your mortgage payments, yearly property taxes, homeowner's insurance, repairs, and utilities.

With the skills this book gives you, you can accurately predict most of these costs and make reasonable estimates about the future. (See Figure I.1.) You also need to keep savings in a bank account, even after you have accounted for these various costs, in order to put food on the table, cover an emergency, and deal with sudden financial changes such as the loss of a job. If, after running your personal financial numbers, you are worried that you cannot afford to purchase a home right away, then rent or stay put where you are.

Mortgage payments
Property taxes
Homeowner's insurance
Repairs
Utilities
Maintenance (painting, landscape, general upkeep, replacements)

FIGURE I.1   Typical Ongoing/Yearly Costs of Ownership of a Home

BUILDING EQUITY

Every homeowner's goal should be to build equity in the home by making mortgage payments and reducing the balance of the loan owed to the lender. To put it bluntly, at purchase most buyers own only a small portion of their home. When a buyer borrows 80 percent of the purchase price, the borrower only has a 20 percent ownership interest in the property. As more and more mortgage payments are made to pay off the loan, the owner acquires a larger and larger ownership interest. Every mortgage payment increases the owner's monetary interest in the home in addition to providing shelter. The way the payments are calculated, however, the early years of payments on the mortgage pay off nearly none of the principal; almost all of those first payments go to the interest. Borrowers making normal payments do not usually build significant equity until the loan has matured for a number of years. However, the exception to this is if they make additional principal payments along with their regular monthly payments.

For renters, on the other hand, you should picture every rent payment you make as your money going into a large trashcan in the backyard to be hauled off by the garbage collectors. Rental payments provide no benefit to you except to provide shelter. Since the government does not encourage renting, tax credits and deductions do not apply to the renter.

As wonderful as homeownership appears, however, if you make the mistake of becoming a homeowner before you can realistically afford the payments, the money put into the home could wind up in that same trash can, along with your hopes for getting a home you really can afford. For a summary of reasons to buy versus reasons to rent, see Figure I.2.

THE CASE FOR RENTING

By renting, you avoid having to make a large down payment to purchase a home plus paying closing costs and inspection and engineer fees. The renter also avoids yearly real estate taxes and the cost of repairs. Also, the renter is free to test different neighborhoods, as renting does not tie the renter to one neighborhood for a long period of

Buying	Renting
Building equity/appreciation	No large down payment
Deduction of interest paid on mortgage and mortgage insurance premiums from federal income tax return	No closing costs
	No inspection fees
	No engineer fees
	No yearly real estate taxes
Deduction of state and local real estate taxes on federal income tax return	No repair costs
Other possible tax deductions	Ability to invest elsewhere and increase savings
Ability to borrow against home's equity and deduct interest owed on federal income tax return	Flexibility to move when lease expires
	No borrowing costs/no mortgage payments
Freedom to personalize home to your preferences	Comparatively risk-free endeavor
Pride in ownership	
Lifetime of shelter	
Security that no one can enter your home without permission	
Possible tax-free capital gain	
Possible long-term wealth	

FIGURE I.2   Reasons to Buy versus Reasons to Rent

time—the typical lease is for the duration of one year. Renting also allows you to practice seeing how much money can be allotted toward paying for a home. Additionally, renting gives you the opportunity to test your saving skills and improve your budgeting abilities. In contrast to purchasing a home, renting is a relatively risk-free endeavor. For a comparison of the initial costs of buying or renting a home, see Figure I.3.

One of my life philosophies is to hope for the best and expect the worst. I avoid gambling. I work too hard for my money to gamble it

Buying	Renting
Down payment	First, and often last, month's rent
Closing costs	
Home inspection fee	Renter's insurance
Initial homeowner's insurance payment	Utilities (sometimes heat and water are included in monthly rent)
Initial mortgage payment	
Homeowner's insurance	Broker's fee, if applicable
Broker's fee, if applicable	

FIGURE I.3   Initial Costs When Buying a Home versus Costs When Renting a Home

away at a casino or in a get-rich-quick real estate plan. In the first decade of the new millennium my conservative anti-gambling theories cost me tons of money. For example, between 2001 and 2002, median home prices shot up in locations all across the United States, demonstrating that a long-term view of real estate may not always be the most profitable. For instance, in Worcester, Massachusetts, the price of a single family home increased by over 25 percent in one year, from $136,000 in 2001 to $170,300 in 2002.

On the other hand, as recent times have demonstrated, the value of real estate can also suddenly decline. As a real estate professional and someone who believes in the longevity of the U.S. economic system, I believe that property will appreciate over the long term but may lose value over the short term. But even if I am wrong, when you purchase a home you at least gain a lifetime of shelter, with the possibility of the home turning into a financial asset that could make your retirement worry-free. Still, in my opinion, anyone looking to purchase a home for less than a five-year time period should rent.

For example, if a buyer purchases a home for $100,000 and decides to sell it three years later and can find only a buyer willing to pay $50,000, then the seller, if he or she accepts that offer, incurs the loss of $50,000, in addition to the continuing interest payments due to the lender until the loan has been satisfied. Also, the *due-on-sale clause* in most mortgages will mean that the $50,000 will require immediate refinancing on the mortgage if, as is generally the case, this person does not have the $50,000 on hand. When attempting to purchase a larger home, you want to avoid having to support two mortgages.

Of course, no guarantee exists that the property will appreciate over many years, but U.S. history thus far supports this principle.

MY STORY: FINDING AND CLOSING ON MY FIRST PURCHASE

During my first purchase I spent many, many hours and months discovering and narrowing down the 10-block radius where I chose to buy. I never made a formal list of my most important housing needs, but I did start exploring different neighborhoods. Being single in 1997, I combined my real estate hunt with my dating life. At a minimum these dates would include dining and walking around the different neighborhoods that I was considering.

I remember my second date with my now friend and client, Rachel (she later married and is happily living with a more normal, great guy named Michael—I represented them in buying their current home). Since New York's Roosevelt Island was underdeveloped, there were deals to be had there. Rachel and I began to learn about the island and its unusual means of transportation, discovering that the most convenient way to enter the island was by a tram. Our date started with a tram ride over the East River. Learning and experiencing everything about Roosevelt Island, from its history of special hospitals for the mentally ill and peculiar former name, Welfare Island, to its current lack of restaurants and grocery stores, made our trek through the island very informative. We attended two open houses and took in as much information as we could absorb. Rachel at least pretended to enjoy the date and hunt. Eventually, however, Roosevelt Island proved not to be my best option.

Price cancelled out many of my top property desires, but I still had many choices within my budgetary means. With a salary of $70,000 at the time, plus the saved profits from my year-old real estate company, BP Vance, I decided that the Upper East Side of Manhattan had the best

(continued)

(*continued*)

value for my money. The big debate in my price range had the beginning of Harlem at the upper end of Fifth Avenue pitted against the urban 50s east of Lexington. Now that I had narrowed down my neighborhoods and spent many hours comparing rates and lenders, I had a budget and narrowed my search accordingly to a number of properties.

Looking back and realizing that the story of my first purchase would be useful for this book, I wish I could have had an easier first-time buying experience, but it took me nine months of looking, including more open houses than I can remember, and heavy negotiations, before I found the one.

I decided to follow and monitor a few properties that I was interested in. Each week I tracked the price changes and kept in touch with the brokers involved, always asking for the lowest price that the seller would accept. I kept different pieces of paper with information on each property, which I updated upon every change. Even before the existence of the digital camera, which has made capturing memories much easier and more commonplace, I had been taking pictures of potential homes and anything that would give me ideas on how I might want to decorate.

To each real estate agent I met at an appointment or open house who seemed interested in me, I gave out my business card and asked them to keep me updated on any new listings within my criteria. If a broker had more than one property I was interested in, I would play the two apartments against each other so that word would get back to the seller that they might lose the sale to another apartment.

My first boss as a lawyer used to tell me not to cry over the deals that I did not make but over those that I did that went bad. So, although I lost out on some good ones, I followed this advice. The brokers on these deals definitely enjoyed letting me know that the homes in question were in contract and off the market. I was determined, however, to get the best deal possible, and I was willing to work hard and be patient enough to suffer the slings of pain.

By now I had become an expert on what type of home I could afford. Due to my budget, my only option on the island of Manhattan was a cooperative unit, so I narrowed down a number of buildings with decent financial statements that would be flexible in accepting a purchaser with limited financial means. I was ready for the kill.

In the final weeks before getting a yes on an offer, I had focused my search on two listings, while also continuing to look for any new entries to the market. Stalkingly, I spent many hours on the second floor of a

McDonald's that had a view of a 57th Street building's apartment. The apartment in question was priced so far out of line with the market that it had been for sale for more than six months. After a number of visits to both apartments, I made an offer well below asking on the 57th Street apartment, hoping that the seller would bite since he probably had not had any offers at the asking price.

My plan worked and the seller accepted the offer. I cherished all 400 square feet of my new home. I spent months choosing the right carpeting, pictures, and frames, as well as showing it off to my friends and family—everyone was offered a place to crash in New York City. Within the same year that I purchased the unit, an apartment of the same size and in the same line of the building sold for over 30 percent more than what I paid, and by 2008 the value of my apartment had skyrocketed by over 400 percent. I lived in this apartment for three years and still own and rent it today.

My hunt for the best home at the best price involved many attributes. My passion for achieving the best in everything and my insistence in putting forth the maximum effort in every task were crucial. Of course, an appreciation for money as a result of growing up with so little of it subconsciously became the music playing in the back of my head. I felt the thrill of the great chase that had brought me to this momentous occasion, which at the time was one of my proudest moments.

Now, I have taken this vigor, my sweat, and worn out shoes, and put them together with the knowledge and experience of experts, to make sure that every homebuyer goes shopping prepared with an extra advantage over all other purchasers.

CHAPTER SUMMARY AND INSIDER TIPS

- The multiple costs involved in the purchase of a home can be grouped into two categories: the costs of taking ownership of a home and the costs of maintaining ownership. The costs of taking ownership of a

(continued)

(*continued*)
home include the down payment, closing costs, home inspection/engineer's fee, initial payments for homeowner's insurance, and the initial mortgage payment. The costs of maintaining a home generally include your mortgage payments, yearly property taxes, homeowner's insurance, repairs, and utilities. All of these costs and fees must be carefully taken into consideration when doing the necessary budgeting to decide whether you can afford to buy a home.

- Many governments provide tax incentives to encourage home buying. You should inquire with local real estate professionals about tax incentives in the state and city or town in which you wish to purchase, and remember to factor these into your to buy or to rent decision.

- If, after doing all of the necessary budgeting, you learn that the cost of owning a home is not something you can currently afford, just keep filling your savings account until you are ready to make your dream come true. It is far better to wait a few more years to be able to afford a home than to buy a home and lose it, possibly destroying your chance to have some other lender take a chance on you again in the future.

- Comparatively speaking, renting is a cheaper alternative to buying a home, and less risk is involved. The renter does not spend the large down payment that a buyer needs to purchase a home, nor does the renter pay closing costs, inspection, or engineer fees. The renter also avoids yearly real estate taxes and the cost of repairs. Moreover, renting allows you to test different neighborhoods, as you are not tied down to one neighborhood for a long period of time.

- Renting can be a good temporary measure for the person who wants to buy eventually but is currently not in the position to do so. By renting in the short term, you will avoid unmanageable debts and will be free to relocate and buy when you are ready to settle down or to make a long-term investment.

- Even if you find that you can afford to buy a home, do not underestimate the importance of keeping extra savings and continuing to save. Even after you have accounted for the various costs of homeownership, you must have additional savings in a bank account in order to provide food on the table, cover emergencies, and deal with sudden financial changes such as the loss of a job.

- In addition to shelter, rental payments provide no benefit to you. Since the government does not encourage renting, tax credits and deductions do not apply to the renter.

One

FINANCE

Do Not Go Shopping Until You Know
How Much Money You Have to Spend

Chapter 1 Get Ready to Buy

Tools and Suggestions to Maximize Buying and Borrowing Power

Traditionally, buying a home in the United States required that a buyer fund 20 percent or more of the purchase price. But over the years, first government-insured home loans and then other types of home loans requiring the buyer to fund only 5 or 10 percent of the purchase price have flourished and are common, even after the real estate crash. By taking out such a loan, a financially stable person can realistically afford to purchase a home. This chapter gives advice on maximizing your ability to obtain a home loan, that is, a mortgage. It will also help you evaluate how much money to spend on a home based on your individual family needs and spending power.

MAKE A LIST OF YOUR ASSETS AND LIABILITIES

Never go shopping unless you know how much money you have to spend.

Start by making a list of your total assets, income, and liabilities. This will provide data that can be easily analyzed by you and by a lender, not only to determine how much money you can comfortably borrow, but also to determine how much of your income will be needed to pay the cost of operation and maintenance of your home. The list will also prove helpful when you complete a lender's application for financing, as well as in preparing a cooperative or condominium application for submission to the board of directors reviewing your financial ability to afford the cost of a home.

Accessible Income

The list's first section should include monies immediately at your disposal, including cash, checking and savings account balances, stocks, bonds, and retirement accounts (IRA and 401(k) accounts). Add to this any gift from a relative or monies from a trust or bequest. These are the funds that you will use to provide the down payment—the amount of money that you will pay for the property to be held until closing by the buyer's attorney, the real estate broker, or the escrow company.

Enduring Income and Other Assets

The second part of the list is made up of your total enduring income, which is the steady income you receive monthly, yearly, or regularly that can be predictably counted. Examples of enduring income include your yearly salary, profits, and the value of any property owned, including the fair market value or listed price of a home to be sold, if any, or the property's rental income if it is an investment property. If applicable, social security or disability benefits, alimony, and monies from a divorce agreement should also be included in this list.

These two parts of the list will show your total income and assets.

Liabilities

The third and final part of the list should be titled *liabilities* and should include every penny of monies you owe to anyone. Separately list both your monthly payments and the total amount of each debt. Liabilities typically include recurring monthly expenses, such as utility bills, insurance payments, charitable pledges, tuition payments, alimony payments, mortgage payments, and any other type of loan, including student and car loans as well as credit card debt.

Proof of Assets

Remember, depending on the type of loan, your lender may need proof of your listed assets. Please see Chapter 2, *How to Get the Cheapest Loan at the Best Rate,* for the details on lenders' requirements. You should therefore collect the necessary documentation of your assets when preparing your list of total assets. For example, lenders usually require three of the most recent monthly bank statements, two years' tax returns, at least one W-2 form (the tax statement your employer is required to provide every year for tax purposes, which summarizes your yearly income), a few recent paycheck stubs proving employment and detailing salary, as well as proof of most of your assets. For proving an existing home's value, an actual listing or an appraisal will usually suffice. If the house is under contract, provide a copy of a signed sales contract. A written separation or divorce agreement can be provided as proof of monies required to be paid to you as a result of a marital breakup.

Use this list when you talk to a lending professional to determine the amount of money you can afford to borrow from a lending institution and your borrowing power.

CREATING A BUDGET AND LIVING WITHIN YOUR MEANS

Once the three parts of the list have been completed you can realistically analyze and determine your buying power. Many financial planners assert that no more than 25 to 33 percent of your salary after tax and other income should be used to pay for the monthly cost of a home. Others preach that you should not spend more than 40 percent of your after-tax income on housing. In New York City, many large apartment building owners rent only to persons whose total income equals 40 times the monthly rent. Instead of embracing a certain formula, I advocate first conducting an analysis of your total income and expenses. By following this path, you will identify your previous spending habits and may be able to eliminate unnecessary items from your future spending. Remember, how much you earn is only relevant after you subtract your necessary expenses. The amount you are able to save is the key.

Together, total income, assets, and liabilities provide an excellent X-ray of your finances. So, we can use these numbers to take a closer look at your monthly spending. You can start with housing, transportation, food, medical/dental insurance, phone, cable, and clothing. Add any other fixed costs such as loans, credit card debt, and car payments. You may want to put as many items as you can on a credit card for a month or two in order to keep better track of your spending habits. Keep a separate tally for your housing expenses.

Track your spending for a few months. Housing, transportation, and food will take up a large chunk of your income. Also note the changes that may be expected in your spending once you own a home. For example, if you are paying rent for your present housing, determine the difference between your estimated mortgage payments, real estate taxes, and other home expenses (fuel, electricity, gas, maintenance) compared to the rent and utilities you are currently paying. Remember that interest paid on your home loan and real estate taxes are tax-deductible but no deduction is allowed for rental payments. Compare the monthly housing expenses and whether, at that level of expense, you were able to save a comfortable amount of money each month. If you are living with your parents or anywhere else where you are not paying rent, consider if there are any other payments that might be eliminated upon the purchase of a new home. Can you give up a car if you move from the suburbs to the city? If you are already an owner, you should be able to afford the difference between the old and new housing expenses.

Once you find the amount you are comfortable spending for your total monthly housing expenses, you will be ready to intelligently shop for a home and choose the proper mortgage.

Your total housing expenses include monies spent through closing and after closing for maintaining a property. The biggest ongoing expenses will likely be the mortgage payments and real estate taxes.

After a conversation with your lending professional, you will have an estimate of the amount of money you will be able to borrow and the monthly mortgage payments necessary to repay the loan. Then include your yearly housing costs such as homeowner's insurance, heating and cooling, electricity, water, repairs, and common charges for a condominium or maintenance for a cooperative apartment. For cooperative apartment ownership, remember that the taxes and part of the mortgage on the building are paid out of monthly maintenance payments. Usually the largest single expense is the down payment amount, which is discussed below.

If your analysis concludes that you need more time to save before buying a home, you should set some saving and spending goals. Your ultimate goal should be not only to create a budget but also to put away as much savings as possible out of your income. Many of my clients have started with a piggy bank. Others have created bank accounts exclusively for deposits to be used only for purchasing property.

MY STORY: BUDGETING AND TRACKING SPENDING

My Grandpa Bob Vance was my most important cheerleader and teacher about budgeting and saving. Grandpa Bob sold picture frames for a living, and he was the richest person I had ever met. I had no idea how to define *rich*, but he had the most beautifully decorated apartment in Encino, California, his car always looked new and, unlike so many others in my world, he never complained about money. During my college years at Rutgers, Grandpa Bob began his long campaign to get me to keep track of every dollar I spent so that I could analyze where my money was going each week. It wasn't until after law school that I actually listened to his advice. He spent countless hours discussing money and business with me, and I can sound off his favorite success sayings as he would repeat them countless times with his deep confident voice. Two of his favorites were: "It is not how much you make but how much you save" and "Fear is false evidence assumed real." Years later I named my real estate company BP Vance, after my grandparents, Bob and Paula Vance. Although 80 years old at the time, my Grandpa loved flying to New York and seeing their names in large white letters on the big green façade.

(continued)

(*continued*)

Grandpa Bob urged me to keep more money in my savings account, and he helped me plan for big ticket items like spring break trips. In fact, it wasn't until I realized how badly I wanted to save a down payment for a home that I finally started tracking my spending. Every time I spent money, an entry went on my yellow pad with the date. Everything I doled out money for was noted: food, laundry, clothes, toothpaste, groceries, books, and even the hot dog from the corner vendor. A few pages into the pad, I separately listed my fixed costs and liabilities, which at the time included my rent and education loan payments. As these would change, so would the entries in my legal pad. Eventually, I created a large stack of pads, and my ability to track forced me to be accountable to myself and motivated me to save money in every way possible.

This simple tracking tool allowed me to focus and track my spending and begin to develop my budgeting. Since I had to acknowledge my spending every time I made a purchase, many times I would think twice before indulging myself with a luxury. Over a few weeks and months I noticed patterns. Still, I decided that some extravagances such as weekend dinners at restaurants, although still not strictly necessary, were nevertheless worthwhile. So this simple method both caused me to save money and allowed me to take my first steps toward realistic budgeting.

Unfortunately, at that time, my budgeting demonstrated that I could not afford a home until I learned how to make more and save more. So I set my goals. A little less than three years later, I became a homeowner.

My method of tracking spending developed before the Internet. As the years progressed and as I taught this method, I watched friends and clients build upon its simple philosophies by using computer spreadsheets and Web tools to track spending and budgeting. It was clear that the yellow pads to which I owed my success were a thing of the past, but Grandpa Bob's wisdom remained timelessly valuable with the newfangled tools available to implement it.

When one friend who had taken my advice showed me her computerized spreadsheets illustrating years of budgeting and spending tracking, I was completely dazzled. Her cross-referencing and graphs were marvels; they were like nothing I had ever seen on paper. For those who wish to use them, there are programs such as Quicken, which are more specifically aimed at money management than generic spreadsheet programs.

But the real point of this story is not that you should use this or that program or should use a yellow pad of paper or a pale green one. By keeping spending records you can, like me, develop the self-control and awareness necessary to get the big items you want without frittering away your resources on the small ones.

You can also combine this method with balancing your checkbook and putting as many items as possible on your credit card as long as the credit card charges are paid in full at the end of every month. While this may seem to be the exact opposite of advice you usually receive, in fact, credit card payments allow you to track your spending without having to pull out paper or a computer. The credit card companies not only provide you with a monthly itemized bill, but most will also give you a quarterly or yearly printout upon request and some of them will even break it down into categories.

When you use a credit card, your money stays in the bank and earns interest for an extra 30 days until you pay off your credit card bill.

Of course, this method only works if you pay your full balance on the credit card every single month as soon as the bill arrives. Be careful not to leave the payment to the last day. Some credit card companies purposely structure their late fees to be far above the legally permissible interest and therefore they actually want you to be late in your payments. But if you pay your full balance as soon as the bill arrives you save a lot of money and also improve your credit score.

Many credit card companies allow a grace period in which no late fee will be imposed after the due date. Be sure to check with your company about this. Also check any programs where you can earn money, airline miles, or other so-called gifts. Of course, they are not really gifts; you are paying for them either with your money or the money of the merchants where you are shopping.

So whether using paper or a computer, Grandpa Bob's saving plan really does work as long as you have the passion to make it a success. As he would tell you with a smile, "You must believe, in order to achieve."

THE DOWN PAYMENT AND PRIVATE MORTGAGE INSURANCE

Today, a down payment usually equals between 5 and 10 percent of the purchase price, depending on the property's location. Newly constructed luxury homes and apartments may require a higher down payment. In many areas, the standard down payment equals 10 percent of the property's purchase price. The down payment is, however, a negotiated number and the state of the market usually dictates the number.

Sellers typically require between 5 and 10 percent of the purchase price not only because attorneys and real estate agents tell them it is the standard, but also because a signed contract means that the home will be taken off the market for a number of months. The possible loss of a buyer's down payment usually eliminates any incentive for a buyer to walk away from a deal. If there is no initial down payment, a buyer may be emboldened by other attractive homes on the market and walk away from the deal despite a signed contract prohibiting such conduct.

Never be afraid to negotiate with a seller to decrease the amount of the down payment. In most cases, the worst that can happen is that the seller will say no. Holding your money in escrow provides very little value to sellers, since it cannot be used until the actual sale or closing occurs. From your perspective, if the closing does not occur because the sellers are waiting for their new home to be built or because of a messy divorce battle over the property, or for a number of other creative reasons, as little money as possible should be tied up.

You, or the seller, may even decide not to close for some reason. If this happens, it benefits you to have contributed as small a down payment as possible as a seller can retain only this amount of the purchase price upon a failure to close, if the property contains less than four units.

Be aware that many lenders and cooperative apartment boards require that you pay at least 20 percent of the purchase price (and sometimes even more) at the closing, but it is rare for them to require a down payment of more than 10 percent of the purchase price.

As a buyer, you can contribute as much money as you desire toward the property at the time of closing and after. You may even overpay your loan payments in order to pay off your home loan earlier than its stated maturity date. However, it is important to be aware that if your loan includes a prepayment penalty (a charge for paying off a loan before a certain date), you may be penalized for paying the loan down before that date. Lenders are required to notify a borrower in writing of a prepayment penalty before the closing, so that you won't be surprised by its existence at closing.

Paying at least 20 percent of the purchase price at closing is necessary to avoid private mortgage insurance (PMI). PMI provides insurance to a lender for homes where the buyer obtains a loan for an amount that is greater than 80 percent of the home's value. PMI charges vary depending on the size of a loan, but typically equal 1/2 of 1 percent of the loan, and this amount is usually paid monthly with your mortgage payment. Except for certain high-risk and delinquent borrowers, and certain VA and FHA loans, PMI mortgage premiums and coverage end when the loan-to-value ratio equals 80 percent or the borrower has paid 20 percent of the value of the loan. Although the Homeowners Protection Act of 1998 requires lenders to automatically cancel PMI upon this occurrence, this does not always happen. So, the borrower should be sure to remind the lender to eliminate this fee at the proper time. Many banks will discontinue PMI upon receiving sufficient proof of increases in market value, such as by an appraisal.

If acceptable to lenders, another popular method to avoid PMI is to structure two loans at closing. For example, buyers who would like 90 percent financing could take out a first loan of 80 percent of the property's value and a second loan for 10 percent of the property's value, thus avoiding the imposition of PMI. Note, however, that when lenders curtail the free flow of money, such a scenario would be difficult to obtain.

OBTAINING A CREDIT REPORT

When planning to purchase a home and take out a loan, one of your first steps should be to order a copy of your credit report. As a result of the Fair and Accurate Credit Transactions Act, a free credit report can be ordered from each reporting agency once a year, online or by phone.

Once you receive a copy of your report, make sure it does not contain any mistakes or incorrectly reported delinquent accounts. All credit reporting agencies provide mechanisms to challenge listed information and you can receive more detailed information by contacting the reporting company. Challenge negative remarks in your credit report, even if they are debatably true. Under federal law, if the company placing the negative remark does not respond within 30 days, the remark must be removed. In response to the challenging of information through hundreds of credit-reporting companies over the years, companies will now often remove negative information for minor defaults with an explanation or reason for the default.

However, companies vigorously seek to protect the reported information for severely delinquent accounts. Whether you are challenging a delinquent report or attempting to correct false information reported, the process can take anywhere from several weeks to several months. Therefore, checking your credit report should be one of the first tasks in the purchase process.

A potential homeowner should have a solid credit history with at least two credit cards (some lenders want to see five credit lines) used at least a number of times a year. Lenders are looking to see a credit history illustrating that the borrower responsibly handles his or her debt obligations by making timely payments. At the same time, too many active credit card accounts can cause the lender to decrease the amount of money they are willing to lend. Because you have access to it, lenders assume that you will use all of the eligible credit available on your cards. So, when determining the amount to be loaned, lenders will subtract from the total approved loan amount the maximum available credit provided to the credit cardholder. Hence if you qualify for a $100,000 loan and the credit card company provides $10,000 as a maximum to use on the credit card, the amount of your loan will probably be decreased by $10,000 to $90,000.

FICO SCORE

Almost all major lenders determine your ability to obtain a loan based on your FICO score (an acronym for Fair Isaac Corporation). A FICO score applies statistical methods to information in a credit report to determine lending decisions, including the interest rate to be charged and the amount of the loan to be offered to a borrower. The highest FICO score is 850 and most people strive to get a score of 720 or above in order to obtain the best interest rate, as any lower score would result in negative rate adjustments, meaning higher interest rates. It is necessary to have a minimum FICO score of around 620 to obtain a loan. It is important to note that when co-borrowers are involved, the bank will usually consider the lowest of the FICO scores in its lending decisions. A FICO score can only be raised by improving your credit report, hence the importance of obtaining a credit report early in the purchasing process.

By following the above suggestions in your pursuit of purchasing a home, you will increase your chances of buying a home you can afford while obtaining the greatest amount of savings and the lowest possible price.

CHAPTER SUMMARY AND INSIDER TIPS

- Open a separate bank account—call it your *saving for a home account*. Combine this with a piggy bank for the same purpose, and put as much money as you can, from a bit of change to a whole paycheck, into both of these funds.
- When close friends and family members ask what gifts they should get you for birthdays and holidays, if appropriate, ask for a donation to the buy-a-home fund. This may seem tasteless, but you might end up with a gift even greater than expected. If a gift is particularly large, you could even offer to name the backyard, a terrace, or other parts of your home after the gift-giver.
- The better organized are your proofs of assets and liabilities, the better your chances of convincing the bank to give you a loan, and having a lender's pre-approval letter handy makes the seller more likely to consider your offer. Remember that the most financially qualified buyer will probably be the one to close on the home.
- Check your credit report long before you start shopping for a home, as it may take months to resolve mistakes and complications.
- Challenge negative remarks in your credit report, even if they are debatably true. Under federal law, if the company placing the negative remark does not respond within 30 days, the remark must be removed.
- It is not how much you earn but how much you save that counts. The person that makes and saves $1,000 is richer than the person that makes and spends $1,000,000.
- Stay away from debt. Americans have a fascination with debt because of the tax deductions involved. But the amount you pay in interest throughout the years usually amounts to far more than the money saved through tax deductions.
- You should always put down as little as possible for your down payment at the time of signing the contract of sale. If you cannot close on your purchase for any reason, you do not want your down payment to become a gift to the seller. You can always add as much as you want at closing.

Chapter 2 How to Get the Cheapest Loan at the Best Rate

HOW BANKS MAKE MONEY BY GIVING YOU A LOAN

Banks typically make the majority of their money from charging interest on loans they give people. Interest is an amount charged on borrowed money; it's usually an annual fee based on a certain percentage—the interest rate—of the total amount of money loaned. In charging you this interest rate, banks usually require payment on a monthly basis. For example, if you receive a 30-year loan for $100,000 at 7 percent interest per year, your total monthly payment for the 30 years would be around $665.30. For the first month, $583.33 of this monthly payment would be interest, and the remaining $81.97 would be a payment against the principal amount owed.

A typical loan requires that the borrower pay back a portion of the money borrowed combined with interest on the total amount borrowed. Figure 2.1 shows the result of the first year of payments on a 30-year fixed-rate mortgage.

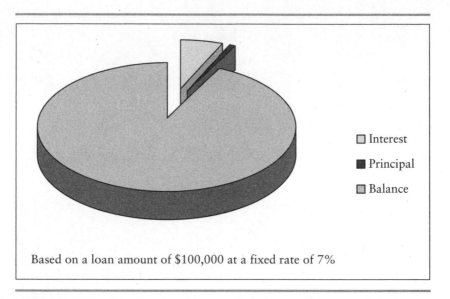

Based on a loan amount of $100,000 at a fixed rate of 7%

FIGURE 2.1   First Year of Payments on a 30-Year Fixed-Rate Mortgage

The isolated slice represents the amount of the year's entire mortgage payment. The large portion of the slice is the proportion of this payment that is interest, and the small portion is the principal.

For interest-only loans, the borrower would, on a monthly basis, pay back only the interest due and nothing against the principal amount of the loan. The principal of the loan would then fall due as a lump sum on the maturation date of the loan.

WHAT IS A MORTGAGE?

When a bank allows you to borrow money, they are betting that you'll be able to pay them back. At closing, the bank will require you to sign a note that serves as a promise to repay the money based on the terms to which you've agreed. In the event that you're unable to make the payments, the bank has additional security in the mortgage—also called a *deed of trust* or *trust deed* in certain states. The borrower signs the mortgage, which permits the lender to take ownership of the property upon a borrower's default in payment. If the borrower does not cure the default, the lender can—through foreclosure—obtain ownership of the property and attempt to make up the loss by selling it to another purchaser.

William Shakespeare wrote, *"What's in a name? That which we call a rose / By any other name would smell as sweet."* This also applies to mortgages. In at least one state, California, the mortgage is called a deed of trust. The difference between a mortgage and a deed of trust stems from the addition of a trustee. With a deed of trust, the lender still loans the money, and the borrower still promises to pay the loan back; however, a third party—the trustee—holds title to the property until the loan is paid off. Like a mortgage, if the borrower defaults, the lender can repossess the home in question.

OBTAINING THE LOAN: LEARNING THE BANK'S REQUIREMENTS

Obtaining a loan from a bank can be similar to going for a job interview. You need to dress appropriately and present yourself as a well-qualified buyer. Whether you have a mortgage broker with you or not, you will have to convince the bank that you qualify for a loan by showing that you can afford to make the payments.

Lenders look at a number of factors to determine whether you qualify for a loan. The bank will first explore how steady your employment is and how much you make annually. They'll also examine any other sources of income, how much money you've saved, and the value of any investments you have. Next, the bank will appraise the home you are trying to purchase to determine its market value. Appraisal ensures that if you default on your payments, the bank can take back the property and resell it for an amount at least equal to the balance due on the loan. The bank then compares your assets with the amount of money you owe creditors pursuant to loans, credit card balances, car leases, or any other outstanding debts. Finally, the bank obtains a credit report to determine your credit score and history of paying bills on time.

The bank will use all of these criteria to decide whether you qualify for a home loan of the amount you've requested.

Lenders traditionally use proportional criteria when deciding whether to grant a loan. For example, if your mortgage payment will be the only debt you carry, many lenders will approve a mortgage with monthly payments of an amount up to 39 percent of your gross monthly income. If, however, you have other debts—such as car payments, school loans, and credit card debt—many lenders may grant a loan for no more than 28 percent of your gross monthly income, depending on the amount of the other debts.

THE MORTGAGE BROKER

Instead of (or in addition to) going to a bank directly, purchasers may also seek a mortgage broker's advice. Many times, mortgage brokers have access to private money or the products of several banks. You may want to compare a mortgage broker's products to those of direct lenders to see who has the better interest rate or price on the life of a loan.

GETTING THE BEST LOAN: FITTING THE LOAN INTO YOUR PLANS AND FINANCIAL MEANS

The most important item to confirm when taking out a mortgage loan should be that you can afford to pay the loan back. Of course, you are shopping for the cheapest loan possible. Once you have figured out how long you plan to stay in the home, the appropriate loan with the lowest interest rate and the lowest fees wins. The Internet has made it much easier to compare one loan to another these days. Ask the lender's loan officer to send you a list of all the fees you will have to pay regarding the loan, along with the interest rate being offered. This information should help you figure out both the loan's monthly cost and total lifetime cost. You will be able to make comparisons between the fees charged by this bank for services, such as title insurance, appraisal, and the bank attorney's charges, to fees other banks charge.

THE NEW GOOD FAITH ESTIMATE: KEEPING THE LENDER HONEST

The law requires the lender to give you a Good Faith Estimate (GFE) of your closing costs in writing. The GFE document will individually list all of the fees you are likely to pay, and it will include an estimated final total figure. Most lenders will have you sign the estimate as proof that you have read and understood it.

Before January 1, 2010, the Good Faith Estimate was just that—an estimate that frequently could not be relied on for accuracy. However, as of January 1, 2010, the federal government implemented new rules to help borrowers better understand a loan's total costs and to ensure that the fees promised at the start of the application process are equal to those charged upon funding the loan. The revised Real Estate Settlement Procedures Act requires that within three days of applying for a federally related loan (which most loans are), the lender must issue a GFE that accurately lists the cost of the loan. The new GFE requires lenders to list all fees that will be charged at closing when they issue the GFE. If costs change for any reason between the GFE's delivery and the closing, a lender may issue a new GFE with these changes without any penalty.

Some of the fees mentioned in the Good Faith Estimate must be identical to the amounts charged at closing. These include those listed for transfer taxes and for the costs of the loan, such as origination fees, points, and the charge for a specific interest rate selected. The sum of the amounts listed for the purchaser's and lender's title insurance and services as well as the governmental recording charges can only increase up to 10 percent at closing when the borrower uses companies recommended by the lender. Very few loan items are unrestricted, including interest rate changes.

To ensure the lenders' accountability at closing, there is another document provided—called a *HUD-1*—which compares the GFE to the final charges. When these charges go beyond permissible limits, the lender must reimburse the borrower for these amounts, or otherwise pay penalties.

CHOOSING THE MOST APPROPRIATE INEXPENSIVE LOAN

How much you enjoy the loan officer's company and smile or which loan officer had the nicer phone voice or office should not affect your decision when choosing a loan. The most important consideration should be your ability to negotiate the loan down to the lowest possible price. Remember, you will no longer be dealing with that loan officer once the loan has been funded. Educate yourself on all the options, and choose the most affordable loan that suits your criteria.

ANNUAL PERCENTAGE RATE (APR)

APR refers to the annual percentage rate, which describes the total price of the loan over its term. If you are getting a fixed-rate loan over a set number of years for which the interest rate cannot fluctuate, comparing one loan's APR to another's should help you determine which is cheapest. If all else is equal, the loan with the lowest APR will be the cheapest loan. However, APR is not always a very good indicator of the cheapest loan because these loans can fluctuate based on prepayment penalties, interest rates, and other fees. Besides comparing the APRs, make sure you obtain a list from lenders of all other fees that may arise over the course of the loan period.

TAX DEDUCTIONS AND THE INTEREST RATE ON YOUR MORTGAGE

If you are eligible to deduct your interest payments on your annual income tax return, then the effective interest rate on your mortgage will actually be lower than what you are paying to the lender.

Real estate attorney Leonard Ritz explains how it works:

> On your income tax return, interest that you pay on your home loan can be deducted from your gross income in order to determine your taxable income. You then pay tax based on your lower taxable income, so you will pay less income tax than you would have paid without the loan.
>
> Assume a household has an income of $150,000, is in a 30% tax bracket, and is paying $25,000 mortgage interest per year at a rate of 5% on a loan of $500,000. But because they can deduct that $25,000 interest payment from their gross income when calculating their income tax, they will save $7,500 in income tax payments (30% of $25,000).

Offsetting the tax savings against their interest payments means that their net after tax interest cost is only $17,500. And that means that the effective, after tax interest rate they are paying on their loan is really only 3.5% ($17,500 divided by $500,000), not 5%.

PAYING POINTS

Sometimes the loan with the lowest interest rate is not necessarily the best choice. One way to decrease an interest rate is to allow the borrower to buy or pay a *point*, which equals 1 percent of the full loan amount. The more points the borrower pays, the lower the initial interest rate paid over the first payment period of the loan. You can usually pay the points up front at closing and deduct them from that year's income taxes. However, doing so will increase your APR. It is crucial that you understand the finances involved in the lending process to be able to make the very best and most educated decision.

You'll want to compare loans both with and without points. Deciding whether or not to take this approach depends crucially on how long you intend to keep the loan before paying it off, by either refinancing or selling. Determine how long it will take for you to break even on the amount that you paid for the points. If this length of time is longer than the period for which you're keeping the loan, paying points will mean a loss, and should therefore be avoided. If, however, you're going to break even with the amount that you paid for the points well within the length of time that you intend to keep the loan, you may decide that paying points would be a wise choice for you. Use a mortgage calculator—(a tool that can be easily found online at my law firm's Web site www.alblawfirm.com or on this book's Web site)—to compare the prices of the loan with and without points and to determine how long it would take to break even on the amount you would pay for the points. You can also do this by using the following formula.

1. Find the figure for the difference between the monthly loan payment if you have paid points and the monthly loan payment if you have not paid points.
2. Take the amount you would have paid for the points and divide this by the figure from the first step.

The figure you come up with will be the number of months it would take you to break even, which will help determine whether you would benefit from paying points.

Figure 2.2 is an example based on a 30-year loan and the assumption that each point purchased reduces the interest rate by 0.25 percent.

In the example, the amount of time it would take to break even with the amount spent on points equals almost 58 months—a little over four years and nine months. If you plan to keep the home loan longer than this, buying points would save you money. If, however, you do not, then paying points would actually end up costing you more.

Loan Amount		$240,000.00
Interest rate		8 percent
Monthly loan charge with interest		$1,761.03
Charge for 2 points	$2,400 (1 percent of loan amount) $\times$ 2 =	$4,800.00
Interest rate with 2 points	8 percent − 0.25 percent − 0.25 percent =	7.5 percent
Monthly loan charge with interest after points		$1,678.11
Difference between monthly loan charge with and without points	$1,761.03 − $1,678.11 =	$82.92 difference per month
Time to break even	$4,800 charge for points/$82.92 difference =	57.887 months to break even

FIGURE 2.2 Time Required to Break Even on a $240,000 30-Year Loan, with and without Paying Points

THE AMOUNT OF THE LOAN

Do not make the mistake that thousands of foreclosed homebuyers did when they took as much money as the bank offered to buy or refinance their homes. In most of these cases, borrowers took for granted that the lender would never give them more money than they could actually afford to pay. They therefore borrowed the maximum allowed—which we all now know led to disastrous consequences.

Buyers need to analyze their own monetary situations in order to determine their steady or continuing income and any other sources of wealth. The borrower should then deduct the amount of money expected to be given to the seller as the down payment as well as subtracting any other debts that need to be paid in the future. Fixed costs, which may include the estimated cost of food, clothing, schooling, transportation, and any other monies that can be predicted to be spent in the future, need to be compared to the budget prepared in accordance with the first chapter of this book. By putting these estimated costs together with the fixed income and liabilities, buyers will be better able to predict how much of a loan they can afford to pay monthly to the bank.

DOCUMENTS REQUIRED TO OBTAIN A LOAN

Among the documents the bank will likely request are your bank statements from the last three months; statements for investment accounts such as stocks and brokerage accounts; recent employment pay stubs; copies of your W-2 forms for the past two years; copies of tax returns; a gift letter (if someone is giving you money to help purchase a home); a copy of the cancelled down payment check; a copy of the contract of sale (for the home you are buying or selling); divorce decree (if any); and any other documents proving your income and liabilities.

THE DIFFERENT TYPES OF LOANS

Loans come in almost as many varieties as ice cream flavors. The goal is always to find the loan that best fits your needs and ability to pay. Discussed in the next sections are a number of different loans that are typically offered to prospective homebuyers. While other types may be created and offered to borrowers in the future, the key to any type of loan is to determine how much money the buyer must pay to the bank monthly, and for how many years. Will the payments remain the same for the life of the loan? Will the interest rate fluctuate based on the condition of the financial market or on some readily ascertainable standard such as, for example, the federally established cost-of-living index?

The Fixed Rate Mortgage

The fixed rate mortgage is the most popular and predictable type of loan. In this scenario, the borrower pays the same interest rate for the loan's entire lifespan. A fixed monthly payment will be applied every month to the principal and interest of your loan. The fixed rate loan options usually provide for a 10, 15, 20, or 30-year fixed rate mortgage.

The Adjustable Rate Mortgage (ARM)

These fluctuating mortgages are called *adjustable rate* mortgages. As many borrowers have found out in the past, monthly payments on such mortgages can rise dramatically to amounts the borrower may not be able to afford, depending on various economic conditions.

For those persons who intend to own the home for a very short time, an adjustable rate mortgage—or *ARM*—may be a highly beneficial way to keep payments affordable. However, adjustable rate mortgages can be ticking time bombs in the case that interest rates greatly increase and the payments reach an amount beyond that which the borrower can afford. Such increases can lead to financial ruin or foreclosure,—or both, since the borrower may not only be unable to make the increased loan payments, but may also not be able to sell the home. ARMs allow a borrower's interest rate to fluctuate according to a certain identified interest rate index. Some forms of these loans have limits on how high the interest can increase, depending on the particular details of the loan program. These loans are ideal for short-term loans or when interest rates are expected to decrease; since the borrower's interest rate decreases as well, the loan becomes cheaper. However, risk-averse homebuyers who plan to keep their homes for more than a year before selling should ardently avoid these loan options.

THE INTEREST-ONLY ARM

Julie Teitel, a mortgage broker, shares her expertise and explains why she decided to take out an interest-only mortgage loan.

It should be noted that during the time period discussed below, the owner's equity in her home increased. Should the value have decreased whereby the value of the home became less than what was owed on the mortgage, refinancing the home would not have been an option. The buyer would have been stuck with a higher interest rate or would have had to bring cash to the table in order to refinance it. Julie's experience is as follows:

> I believe interest-only mortgages are only good in certain cases: when buyers plan on keeping the mortgage for a short term—approximately less than five years. I actually just sold my apartment that I purchased through an interest-only mortgage. I believe my situation is a perfect example of a situation in which an interest-only mortgage proved most beneficial, since I bought my apartment in May 2003 and sold it in September 2009, 64 months later.
>
> My mortgage loan was for $1,100,000 with an interest rate of only 4.5 percent. The loan itself was a 10-year/30-year ARM, given this title because after 10 years, it has the potential to go up or down every year for the next 20 years. There are ceilings and floors that keep the rate from going too high or too low.
>
> For 10 years, I would have been able to pay an interest rate no higher than 4.5 percent. At the same time in 2003 while I had a 4.5 percent interest rate, those persons who had a 30-year fixed rate mortgage would have paid 5.88 percent in interest. Under the 4.5 percent interest-only rate, I paid $4,125 a month, whereas a person with a 30-year fixed mortgage would have paid $6,510 a month. Therefore, the monthly savings of my interest-only loan compared to the standard 30-year fixed

(*continued*)

(continued)
> rate mortgage was $2,385, and the savings per year of having
> an interest-only loan equaled $28,620.00.
>
>   Since I sold my property within the 10 years that my interest
> rate remained at 4.5 percent instead of holding on to it for a
> longer period where the interest rate would have increased, an
> interest-only loan turned out to be my best option.

The Two-Step Mortgage: 5/25 and 7/23 Loans

Among the most popular types of mortgages during the last decade
is the two-step mortgage, also known as the *5/25* and the *7/23
mortgage*, which are 30-year loans. A 5/25 loan has a fixed interest
rate during the first five years. At the end of this period, the loan
becomes a 25-year adjustable rate mortgage. Alternatively, some programs actually require that the loan be paid off after the initial five-
year period even though its monthly payment is calculated as if the
borrower will pay off the loan over a 30-year period. To continue
the loan under this program, the borrower must still occupy the
property and have complied with all conditions of the loan during
the first five years.

A 7/23 loan works in a similar fashion. However, instead of becoming an adjustable rate loan that can change depending on market
conditions after the first set period, the loan converts to a 23-year
fixed rate mortgage set at the end of the initial 7-year term. A 7/23
loan provides a fixed interest rate for the first seven years. Borrowers
who expect interest rates to decrease after this 7-year term often
choose this type of loan. The loan then locks into a set rate for the
rest of the 23-year loan period. Therefore, borrowers of this type of
loan are gambling that the interest rate set will be lower than for the
original loan after the first seven years. But seven years is a long
time—and rates can increase.

The primary reason for a borrower to take either of these kinds of
loans is to obtain a low interest rate for the first five or seven years.
The bank tends to provide a much lower interest rate in agreeing to a
5- or 7-year fixed term than they do for a 30-year loan. Since many
borrowers may fear not knowing what the interest rates will be after

the first period, they opt to refinance once this initial term runs out, and they enter into a fixed-rate long-term loan instead. Similarly, borrowers selecting the 5/25 loan are betting that interest rates will stay low for the first 5 years while decreasing for the 25-year remainder of the loan when the interest rate becomes adjustable and therefore fluctuates based on market conditions.

The Balloon Mortgage

Balloon mortgages can be for any length of time—generally for 5, 7, or 10 years—and usually contain regular monthly payments. They differ from standard residential mortgages in that at the end of the loan's term, a large percentage—sometimes even the entire loan balance—becomes due and payable in full. In some instances, these loans are set up as interest-only payments.

The No Money Down Mortgage

Another very popular loan (until 2008) was the no money down loan, which finances the full purchase price of the home, including the down payment. The housing crisis has virtually eliminated no money down mortgages as banks' favorite loan products. The banks that still offer these loans usually require you to have up to 20 percent of the purchase price in other assets besides cash—such as stocks, bonds, retirement accounts, or other means of wealth—and the bank will hold these assets as collateral. However, if these assets' values decrease, you may have to come up with the money immediately.

The No Doc Loan

The no documentation loan is another endangered species of loan as a result of the housing crisis. This type of loan allows people to borrow without having to prove employment, income, or assets. No documentation loans normally involve a higher interest rate than traditional loans, and some statement of income and assets would still have to be verified by the bank.

The FHA Insured Loan

An FHA insured loan is a mortgage loan insured by the Federal Housing Administration. Lenders are more likely to approve prospective borrowers in these cases, since the FHA has agreed to insure the loan against the borrower's default. This kind of loan can be obtained by any individual who qualifies, whether a first-time buyer or a current homeowner. Those with a less-than-perfect credit history or a previous bankruptcy will find it easier qualifying for an FHA insured loan than for a standard loan, since a minimum FICO score of just 620 is required.

This loan type also benefits prospective buyers who cannot afford the traditional 10 percent down payment of a standard loan, since an FHA insured loan requires a down payment of around only 3.5 percent. However, borrowers are required at closing to pay an up-front insurance premium typically equaling 1.75 percent of the loan amount, and must pay for Mutual Mortgage Insurance (MMI) for the life of the loan. FHA insured loans can be fixed rate or adjustable rate mortgages, with limits that vary depending on the state, location, and type of property. One drawback to the FHA insured loan is that these cap limits can be quite low in some areas.

The primary reasons to choose the FHA over traditional loans with similar interest rates are the lower down payment and flexible lending policies. Otherwise, the additional fees at closing and the required continued MMI costs can make the FHA an expensive option. The MMI insurance is usually roughly equivalent to the PMI insurance that's charged when a buyer has paid less than 20 percent of the property's value—except the PMI charge disappears once the borrower obtains 20 percent equity in the home, whereas the MMI insurance does not expire until the loan is paid off.

People who are interested in obtaining an FHA insured loan should speak to a number of FHA approved lenders to find the best loan for their needs.

The VA Loan

The VA loan is a mortgage loan guaranteed by the U.S. Department of Veterans Affairs. This loan type is available only to veterans who have met the minimum service requirements, and to widows of soldiers as well. The VA loan does not require any down payment, nor does it require the borrower to obtain Private Mortgage Insurance (PMI). As with the FHA insured loan, the maximum VA loan amount varies with location, and can be obtained only through qualified lenders.

THE LOAN PROCESS

A loan officer or processor guides you through the mortgage process step by step. He or she will take all of your information and create your loan application. The loan processor assists the loan officer by setting up your appraisal and ordering both your credit and title report. This entire process should take three to six weeks, and it will be on the longer end when interest rates become very low, money is tight, or some other factor causes many people to apply for loans within the same time period. Most lenders require you to provide proof of income and assets at the beginning of the application process; once the lender has these documents, the borrowing process usually becomes more efficient.

Private Mortgage Insurance

Also known as PMI, private mortgage insurance is usually required by the lender when you pay less than 20 percent of the purchase price toward the home. PMI will help you to buy a home if you can only contribute a small amount toward your down payment. The PMI provides additional insurance to protect the lender from individuals who default on their loans.

There are ways to cancel your PMI after you have begun paying it. Once your home has reached the 20 percent equity threshold, or your principal payments have reached the 20 percent threshold, you may request that the lender cancel the PMI. Even if you don't make this request, the lender is required to cancel the PMI once you have hit the 22 percent equity threshold. Instead of paying more money to the bank to meet the 20 percent requirement, you may want to have your property reappraised to show that your payments toward the loan equal 20 percent or more based on market conditions alone. In these cases, PMI insurance should be cancelled and PMI payments ceased. As mortgage banker Brian Scott Cohen frequently remarks, "Do not expect the bank to remember to cancel your PMI payments once you have a 20 percent equity position in your property. You should notify your bank both orally and in writing to request confirmation that the payments have ceased."

THE FINANCING PROCESS

The Commitment Letter

Until a commitment letter has been issued, signed by you, and returned to the lender, the bank can withdraw any promise to fund the loan at any time. Therefore, the commitment letter is the key to unlocking the loan's door. However, even a commitment letter may contain conditions that must be satisfied before the loan can close. The most common condition is receipt by the lender of a satisfactory appraisal of the property. I have taken some of my client-buyers' most common questions about loan financing and answered them here to assist in ensuring a better understanding of the process. Additionally, insider suggestions are discussed to assist you in closing on your uncommon deal flawlessly. Once you have received your loan commitment letter, you should immediately send it to your attorney.

Often conditions include anything from proof of employment, proof of ownership or sale of another property, and copies of licenses, to paying off certain debts at closing.

Additionally, you should ask the lender what attorney will be representing the lender at the closing if it is not indicated on the loan commitment letter. You need this information so that your attorney can send a copy of the title insurance report (or the lien search) to the lender's attorney along with a copy of the contract of sale.

Floating the Rate or Locking In

During the application process, you may choose to call your loan officer between the time you apply and the time you close in order to lock in the rate. If you are scheduled to close within 30 days after your application and you feel that rates may drop during that time, you may wait until they drop and telephone to lock in the rate immediately. If they do not go down, you may be stuck with a higher rate. This process is called *floating the rate*.

If you do not choose to float the rate, you can lock it in at the time of your application. It is wise to do this if you are not sure that rates will go down anytime soon. You can hold the lock anywhere from 30 to 60 days. However, the longer the rate is held, the more it will cost you. Therefore, it is very important to get all required documents to the lender as fast as possible.

Understanding Insurance and Tax Escrow

Once you get a loan and buy a home, you are not the only person to have an investment in the property. By signing the document titled *mortgage*, you are assigning your rights in the property to the bank upon a default in payment.

Americans have a saying that nothing is certain in life but death and taxes. As every American town, city, and county depends on property taxes for revenue, your bank wants to ensure that you pay your taxes. For most loans, the bank will bill you for the monies to pay for the home's taxes and insurance, and then pay it on your behalf.

It is in the bank's interest to ensure the timely payment of taxes. The bank does not want to lose the ability to foreclose or take your home from you upon your failure to make mortgage payments. At the same time, the bank desires to protect the value of its pledged asset by ensuring that homeowner's insurance has been maintained. For example, if a fire or storm damages the property, provided that the home is properly insured these repairs should be covered by the insurance.

Knowing that the government gets paid first in a foreclosure proceeding and the failure to pay taxes results in a foreclosure by the government, it is in the bank's interest to have you establish a tax and insurance escrow for these payments. This is why in most cases the bank will require you to maintain a tax and insurance escrow account.

How the Insurance and Tax Escrow Account Works   At closing the bank takes a few months of taxes and insurance payments and retains those payments in an escrow account. This money, which is referred to as *a cushion*, is an excess amount held by the lender in case the tax or insurance bill increases. Every month thereafter, you will contribute a designated monthly amount of tax and insurance payments toward your escrow account. This payment is taken in addition to your mortgage payment, and will be paid into your escrow account on your behalf by the lender.

Additional Considerations on the Insurance and Tax Escrow Account   Although most loans include these escrow accounts, which many times are regulated by federal and state laws, do not be shy about asking the bank to waive the tax and insurance escrow. In many cases the bank will oblige, but understand that if you do waive the tax and insurance escrow account, the bank may charge a slightly higher interest rate, such as 0.25 percent more. Note also that the bank is less likely to waive the tax and insurance escrow if you have paid for less than 20 percent of the home's selling price.

In any event, if you are interested in waiving the insurance and tax escrow account, you should inquire about whether this option is available to you and about any increases in interest rates that may apply.

MY STORY: A LESSON IN OBTAINING A BANK LOAN

I pride myself on not losing my temper. In fact, I claim to raise my voice only about four or five times a year. Knowing that no one ever wins an argument by yelling, and that it certainly does not make friends, explaining and teaching are my favored methods of persuasion. However, a number of years ago, at the very start of my career, applying for one loan had me setting new records for my vocal chords.

Looking back, my experience stemmed from a number of issues. The bank's failures both to communicate clearly and to help me understand the necessary steps to fund the loan were two contributing factors to my resulting stressful experience. My inability to understand the lending process and its rules didn't help the situation either. I now see that it was partly my failure to spend more time collecting references and learning about the lender's different products that laid the foundation for this unfortunate situation. I had also set the wrong ground rules from the start. I was so determined to find the lender offering the cheapest rate for a 30-year fixed rate loan, that without doing the proper homework, I shunned all other programs, loan types, and options, including the opportunity to pay points in order to have a lower interest rate.

Starting my search for a lender after signing the contract of sale was also an unwise decision. As was typical in my locale, my contract of sale only allowed me 30 days to receive a loan commitment from a bank. Not knowing how frequently interest rates changed until the issuance of a commitment letter, I went berserk when I was told the loan's interest rate had increased the day after my appraisal check was cashed. I accused the bank of using bait and switch tactics. To make matters worse, the bank's representative—after waiting a few days to return my call—maintained that this higher rate was actually the one that was initially quoted. Unfortunately, since I didn't have documentation of the original quote, it was his word against mine—and he was in the position of power.

When choosing my lender, although I inquired with all of my connections in the lending business, I decided to go with a bank I had only seen in connection with one deal at the firm where I was working at the time. Foolish as it sounds, I chose them even after seeing how difficult they had been on that one deal. The most important factor in my decision was that the bank in question had the lowest interest rate compared to the other lenders and mortgage brokers I had interviewed. In addition, because I knew the representative and believed he would think I had the potential to refer business, I thought I had made a safe bet. Because of my familiarity with working with this representative, I wrongly chose not to obtain another referral for a different representative. With my application completed and a check for the appraisal cashed, I had foolishly committed to that bank.

Adding to my woes, my credit report listed two late payments, potentially increasing my interest rate, and therefore necessitating that I clear these in record time. Since these negative marks were a mistake, I spent hours on the phone with another bank, faxing them cancelled checks showing my payments had been made on time. I had actually paid six monthly payments in advance, marking each check with a different month. Despite my explicit instruction in writing regarding how these payments should be applied, the bank failed to properly apply them and falsely reported my apparent tardiness to the credit agencies. I had to call the supervisor of the district manager of the bank that reported these

(continued)

(*continued*)

alleged late payments, leave voice mails for the president of the company, and speak to his secretary three times before the bank would sign documents clearing the negative remarks on my credit report. I immediately forwarded the documentation that cleared the negative remarks on my credit report to the credit agencies.

Collecting documents proving the then current amount of my law school loans became the next obstacle, shortly followed by having to prove I was not one of the several persons sharing my name who had judgments against them throughout the country.

With my commitment letter finally in hand, I thought the wind was at my back, and attempting to schedule myself a closing date should have been a technicality. However, my loan officer's weeklong disappearance complicated the situation. Only by calling the main 800 number did I find out that the officer was still alive and breathing. When I did finally reach him, he apologized profusely. The unpleasant surprises did not stop there either. The closing costs collected by the bank appeared outrageous at the time. However, the loan did close, and the market value of the property has, since the day of the closing, almost tripled.

I realized that much of the blame for this unpleasant financing experience lied solely with me. I never should have worked with an unrecommended loan officer. I also should have requested a free credit report from any of the major credit reporting companies the minute I started looking for a property. A loan's interest rate changes frequently, and should only be considered fixed after the lender officially locks in the interest rate for you — something of which you have proof in writing. Thanks to the recent evolution of e-mail and the revised Good Faith Estimate, it is much easier to obtain records of all agreements nowadays—including the interest rate and any other estimated closing fees. I failed to ask for all loan-related costs in writing, and I didn't compare the benefits of different loans or complete a mathematical comparison to see whether I should pay points to lower my long-term payments. Finally, I failed to obtain my lender representative's personal contact details and thus was left in the dark at a crucial point in the lending process.

Adversity's ability to be such a good teacher has allowed this to become a terrific lesson, not only for myself but also for my clients and the readers of this book. As Winston Churchill said, "Success is going from failure to failure without loss of enthusiasm." However, it is my hope that you will benefit from the lessons I learned in order to avoid similar bitter experiences and can instead maintain enthusiasm throughout the entire home buying experience.

Insider Lessons from My Story:

1. Obtain a credit report as soon as you know you want to purchase a home.
2. Use referrals to find a lender.
3. Begin your search for a lender BEFORE signing the contract of sale.
4. Get your interest rate and all other important information in writing.
5. Obtain your lender/bank representative's personal contact details, including his or her cell phone number.
6. Understand that interest rates constantly change. When you believe the time is right, lock in your rate.

CHAPTER SUMMARY AND INSIDER TIPS

- Never go shopping until you know how much you have to spend. Once you know your budget, start calling lenders to both shop for a loan and learn about the different products available.
- No bank will give you a loan commitment without an executed contract of sale. Once the contract has been executed, you should immediately work on obtaining financing
- If you aren't sure, assume that you'll maintain the loan for many years and get a fixed-rate mortgage. Very few things cause greater anxiety than worrying about whether you can afford to make your mortgage payments and if you will lose your home. While variable rate mortgages can seem like a bargain at first, they carry the danger of increasing monthly payments to a point you cannot afford.
- Make lenders compete for your business. Call at least two and let them know you will be comparing products from other lenders. This should motivate them to provide you with their best products at the lowest interest rates and costs.
- If necessary, look for a guarantor—someone who assures your financial obligations, taking legal responsibility upon him or herself. Family members and very close friends may provide the ability to purchase a home. This becomes especially important after a recent job loss, which can frequently become a death sentence to a loan application.
- As long as the interest on your mortgage is greater than you could make from your savings account, stock portfolio, or other investments,

(continued)

(continued)

spend as much money as you can on paying down your mortgage. The interest you pay on a mortgage is many times higher than the interest you get from a checking or savings account at the bank or other financial investments. Therefore, you could be saving more money by paying down your mortgage than you would through receiving dividends in the bank. Of course, always keep a safety net so that you will have enough savings to get you through the rainy days if a job loss or emergency occurs.

- There is no rigid answer as to whether you should pay points. Do the math, figure out your break-even point, and make a decision based on how long you intend to keep the home. Since this method requires that you pay for the points up front upon obtaining the loan, even if the math suggests buying points, do not purchase the points if you do not have the money to pay for them. Never take out a loan for more than you can afford to spend, and always make sure you keep enough savings to prepare for emergencies.

- The contract of sale may give you a period to rescind the contract if you cannot get a loan within a certain time. Make sure you are completely familiar with the terms listed in the contract of sale and that you abide by them. Sellers may even extend the period of time for you to obtain financing if your request is timely. Note, however, that if you cannot obtain financing and fail to alert the seller within the specified time, not only will the seller be able to keep your down payment, but they might also be able to sue you for the difference between the contracted purchase price and the eventual lower price of an actual sale to someone else.

- When comparing bank products, obtain information in writing about everything,—including interest rates, loan amounts, and bank fees. Keep all records of communications so that there are no mistakes about loan rates and charges.

- Too many lenders continue to charge PMI long after borrowers have 20 percent or more equity in the property. Stay on guard and ask for this charge to stop once you have reached the 20 percent mark. To attempt to reach 20 percent equity and terminate the PMI fee if you have not already reached this mark, you should have your property appraised when property values increase.

- Only choose an FHA loan when you cannot afford to pay the higher down payment amount required in other loans, as the additional fees at closing and the continued MMI charges usually make this an expensive loan option.

Chapter 3 Buying a Home with Little or No Money Down and Obtaining Seller Financing

Capitalism makes for the most creative vehicles for transferring land. The engine for this creativity is need. While buyers need a place to live, sellers may need to pay off a mortgage, move to a bigger house, make a profit, or perhaps even do all of the above. The more desperate a seller becomes, the greater a buyer's chances of handing over little money in exchange for a home. The methods discussed below do not apply to transactions where financing will be received from third party private lenders, but rather from the sellers themselves. Using governmental and private lending programs with little or no money down options may result in higher fees, but otherwise they follow the traditional guidelines in the financing chapter of this book. We are therefore talking about owner financing here.

PUTTING LITTLE OR NO MONEY DOWN

Desperate times can lead sellers to especially desperate measures. Of course, every seller would prefer to have the buyer's down payment made at the signing of the contract of sale and for the full purchase price to be paid at closing. But that does not always happen. Sellers cannot rely on receiving a down payment in a weak real estate market; however, many still manage to sell their homes in their preferred price range. In a weak real estate market, buyers who would not normally qualify to reach their goal of homeownership can leverage the market's down conditions to buy a home with little or almost no money down.

For little money down deals with federal government financing or other third party lenders, the fees may be higher but many of the terms remain the same as in any market transaction.

To put little or no money down on a deal with seller financing, you may need to be more willing to negotiate on other terms, such as the purchase price, the interest rate, and the condition of the home. Because negotiating on such terms will not usually be to your advantage, you should only seek such a deal if you are unable to purchase the home with money down or if you are a home investor using other people's money to make a profit from flipping, reselling, or renting the properties purchased.

Some investors use the no money down strategy without even asking the seller to give them a mortgage. They obtain the money to pay for a loan or to take out a second loan based on the equity or value of the home being purchased, or even from the equity or amount that can be borrowed from another home that they may own. These methods are extremely risky and only experienced investors or those with a high level of risk tolerance should use them under the guidance of qualified advisors who have completed these types of deals before.

The anatomy of the little or no money down deal requires the seller to finance your purchase of the property in exchange for your agreeing to pay equal to or above the asking price—and many times, to also pay an above-average interest rate on the loan that the seller provides to you. Instead of paying rent to an owner and receiving nothing aside from immediate shelter for your payments, the no money down purchase allows these monthly payments to go toward paying off the purchase price. Rather than monthly rent, these become mortgage payments.

The Little or No Money Down Negotiation and Process

The essence of the little or no money down negotiation starts with teaching the seller why it is a good idea to accept your offer to purchase the home with little or no money down and with the seller personally financing the transaction. If you fail to make the promised monthly payments, the seller can recover the property and put it on the market again. Once you explain this concept to the seller this may help to soothe his or her fears of the risk involved in this type of transaction. Also, you should promise the seller that as soon as you have enough savings, improved credit, or garner enough equity in the house, you will attempt to obtain a conventional mortgage from a traditional bank.

When sellers possess their own loans and mortgages that they want to pay off, it is even harder to convince them to fund your purchase. For states where they're used, an attorney should be involved as soon as you obtain an accepted offer. In desperate situations especially, your scam radar should be raised. So, a qualified attorney can prove essential in completing the deal. The seller may not want to pay for an attorney, but either way it remains extremely important for you to have your own attorney to make sure that you obtain absolutely clear possession of and title to the land. For information on how to select your attorney please refer to Chapter 14, *Finding and Utilizing an Aggressive Attorney.*

When buying a home with little or no money down, it remains extremely important to follow the suggestions in this book that apply in every type of home purchase. This especially includes securing an engineer or inspector to analyze the home's physical makeup. Budgeting is even more important in home purchases with little or no money down; it is crucial for you to have a thorough understanding of your finances and what you can afford before entering into this type of purchase. As important, you must be aware of the continuing costs of carrying a home, such as real estate taxes and repairs. Do not throw money away for the sake of calling yourself a homeowner. Again—if you cannot afford the payments, then rent and save your money until you can afford to do so properly.

Earning Credibility and the Seller's Trust

This type of negotiation usually goes much more smoothly when dealing with relatives or friends who understand your personal financial situation. When dealing with strangers, explain that you are both cash and mortgage poor and back this up with credible reasons. As sympathetic as you want your situation to seem, you also want to appear responsible enough to convince the seller to take a gamble on you. Give reasons for any poor credit—whether it was the unfortunate adventures of your youth, the loss of your job, the divorce that left you with nothing, the bad business venture, or whatever truth applies. At the same time, make sure that you separate your past misfortunes from the present day. Today you have a steady job and are reliable. In the past, you were unlucky. Many sellers will be willing to root for and assist you as the underdog to reach your dreams; you just have to persuade them that the bet on you is a reasonably safe one.

The Anatomy of the Deal

Avoid trying to negotiate a cheaper purchase price for the property. Remember that you are asking the owner to give you the property in return for future payments, and are attempting to obtain homeownership that you are otherwise not able to afford. You will be turning your rent payments into ownership equity, so you should offer to pay at least the asking price for the property—if not more—to seal the deal. This approach is your best chance of capturing the seller's attention. The seller will want to hear you out for at least a few moments to learn why you want to pay the full asking price or more.

In exchange for your paying the full price, the seller will act as your bank. You will make monthly payments to pay for the entire property, and will need to figure out how many months it will take you to pay off the mortgage loan that the seller is personally providing. Of course, the shorter the time you offer for the payoff period, the better your chance of convincing the seller to go along with it. Make sure that you agree to an affordable price and a reasonable payoff time period so that the owner does not wind up taking the property back.

Make it clear to the seller that you will agree to put all terms in writing, including how fast you will move out of the property if for any reason you cannot afford to make the payments. The personally obtained mortgage from the seller—which in some states is called *the purchase money mortgage*—has given hundreds of thousands of buyers their first homes. While it is not the most common method of purchasing a property, it is still a method that many buyers credit for having allowed their dreams to come true.

MY STORY: BUYING A HOME WITH NO MONEY DOWN

Peter always admired his father-in-law, Jerome, and aspired to have a life just like the one Jerome had obtained. Like Jerome, Peter became a teacher and married another teacher, Lorna. To fulfill his dream, he wanted to own a home just like the one Jerome owned in the suburbs. Though both Peter and Lorna were in love with the house and the town in which it was located, they unfortunately found—based on the prices of similar homes in that area—that they would not be able to comfortably afford the traditional down payment at the time they were looking to move.

Retired from teaching and desiring to live upstate permanently, Jerome, and Lorna's mother, Amy, were actually looking to sell their suburban property. They became discouraged when they learned how prices had crashed and how slowly homes moved on and off the market in their town. But paying taxes for two homes was not an option on two teachers' retirement plans and occasional tutoring and substituting. Jerome and Amy also wanted to rent a place in the city to spend more time with their children.

Since I knew all the parties involved, I came up with a plan that I believed would benefit everybody. Peter and Lorna could purchase Lorna's parents' home with no money down and make monthly payments on a personal loan from Jerome and Amy. Although Peter and Lorna had difficulty saving for a down payment to purchase a home on his salary and tutoring jobs, he and his wife had perfect credit and could easily make the monthly payments. In fact, Peter would be paying almost the equivalent of his current rent for his apartment in Queens, New York

(continued)

(*continued*)

through his monthly home payments. Peter and Lorna's payments would slowly pay down the loan over 30 years.

Peter and Lorna would become homeowners in a beautiful neighborhood, while Jerome and Amy could retire to the country and rent a place in the city, paid through the monthly payments received from their daughter and son-in-law. To top it all off, Jerome and Amy got out of the deal without having to pay a broker or trouble themselves with open houses and strangers tramping through their home.

Without this arrangement, Peter and Lorna would still be renting today. And Jerome and Amy could still be paying taxes on two properties. Everybody except brokers came out ahead on this deal.

This past December everyone became doubly blessed as Lorna gave birth to a baby girl named Isabella Rose.

CHAPTER SUMMARY AND INSIDER TIPS

Finding Your Little or No Money Down Home

- Do the necessary budgeting to figure out exactly how much you can comfortably afford to spend on the home purchase. Looking at what you could pay in rent is the best vehicle for determining what you can pay the seller each month in a purchase where you are not putting any money down and are obtaining seller financing. However, owning a home will incur additional costs such as insurance, property taxes, maintenance, and repairs, which must also be considered in your budget.

- As far as furnishing your new home, make sure you at least have enough money for a bed, and most likely, a couch. However, frugal purchasers understand that the entire home does not need to be furnished in one day. America's third president, Thomas Jefferson, took 40 years to build and rebuild his own home, called Monticello, in Virginia.

- When you visit potential homes, try to get a feel for how desperate the seller is to sell, as desperate sellers may be more willing to accept a little or no money down transaction.

Coming to an Understanding with the Seller

- Once you find the home you would like to purchase and can afford, approach the seller with your offer. Start by explaining why it is a good idea to accept your offer to purchase the home with little or no money down and, if applicable, with the seller also personally financing the transaction.

- You will also need to explain why you are unable to afford the traditional down payment amount and/or to qualify for a traditional loan. Inform the seller that although you are cash/mortgage/credit deficient, you have credible reasons for this and are now a fiscally responsible person.

- Assure the seller that should you fail to make the promised monthly payments, he or she will be able to recover the property and put it back on the market. The seller should know that you would put all terms in writing, including how quickly you would move out of the property if for any reason you could not afford to make the payments.

- You can also promise the seller that as soon as you have enough savings, improved credit, or enough equity in the home, you will attempt to obtain a standard mortgage from a traditional bank.

The Negotiation

- Avoid trying to negotiate a cheaper purchase price for the property. Remember: You are asking the owner to give you the property in return for future payments, and you are attempting to obtain home-ownership that you would not otherwise be able to afford. For such benefits, offer to pay at least the asking price—if not more—in order to seal the deal.

- If you are seeking seller financing, you can also expect or even offer to pay an above-average interest rate in exchange for the seller's loan. However, make sure that you agree to an affordable price and a reasonable payback time period so that the seller does not wind up taking the property back.

- Contact an attorney that has experience representing buyers in little or no money down home purchases as soon as you receive an accepted offer. It is extremely important for you to have your own attorney to make sure that you obtain absolutely clear possession of the land.

Two

FINDING THE UNCOMMON DEAL ON A HOME

Chapter 4 Becoming an Expert on Finding the Dream Home

In order to become an expert on the home buying process, you must acknowledge and respect the fact that information makes the buyer. Treating a potential home as if it will be the greatest purchase of your lifetime and, at the same time, the place you want your friends and/or family to spend some of the most important moments of their lives should result in a fabulous decision.

When looking for a home, start by selecting your preferred location. Becoming an expert means understanding the real estate market within a certain distance, whether it is 10 or 5 miles or just a block's radius. Look at the listings on the Internet or in newspapers. A buyer should actually see several properties before making an offer on a home. By the time your search is completed, you will be able to identify which preferences and dislikes are most important to you—a larger backyard, a swimming pool, or the local school system, for example. Among the topics of your search should be the local schools, places of worship, access to transportation and your workplace, health clubs, shopping, and the security of the area. Prospective neighbors will usually be extremely happy to give advice on all of these topics. Limit your search to properties within your budget, and maybe even a little above your budget in case you are able to negotiate a lower purchase price.

Once you have selected a neighborhood, you should start spending more time in the general vicinity to determine if you are comfortable with the location. It is also important to pay attention to the sounds and smells of the neighborhood; take note of trains, traffic, planes overhead, and local eateries. For most buyers, the community constitutes an important factor in buying a home. Making visits to shops and restaurants and participating in cultural activities are also good ideas.

THE REAL ESTATE BROKER

Real estate brokers and agents make their living by placing people in homes. They are essentially salespeople; they do not get paid unless they sell. Typically, the seller pays the broker's commission, which customarily equals 5 or 6 percent of the purchase price, even though the commission may be divided between two brokers. Since a large portion of the homes for sale are sold by real estate brokers, hiring a broker that works for the buyer—generally called a *buyer's broker*—will not affect a home's sale price. At no time would the buyer have to pay the buyer's broker; customarily, the seller pays the commission to their broker, who then splits it with the buyer's broker. For a detailed discussion of the real estate broker, please see Chapter 5, *Conducting the Search: Finding Your Allies in the Real Estate Hunt.*

FINDING A PROPERTY TO PURCHASE: VARIOUS CHOICES AND FORMS OF SHELTER

In many parts of the country, the different purchasing options and forms of ownership require sophisticated knowledge to enable a buyer to become familiar with various ownership structures and make a wise purchase decision. This chapter provides some basic education on the various types of shelter and homeownership. I will help you wade through the many types of homes to find the one that is most suited to your needs.

The Traditional House and Townhouse

The traditional single family house stands on a plot of land separated from other plots of land. Normally, a buyer owns the house on the property as well as the land it sits on, along with mineral and sky rights under, on, and above the land. Other types of homes contain more than one dwelling unit; these are the traditional two-, three-, and four-family homes. Typically, in these types of houses, one person or couple owns the property, lives in one of the units, and leases the remaining units.

To demonstrate or assume legal ownership of a home, a buyer records a document from the previous owner called a *deed evidencing ownership*. The owner's responsibilities include payment of all utilities, property taxes, and sewer charges, as well as general upkeep of the house and grounds.

Single family homes come in all shapes and sizes, with varying numbers of bedrooms, bathrooms, and even kitchens. Before you proceed, you must establish your minimum requirements.

Townhouses are usually a series of single (or multi-story) homes that are attached to each other horizontally. As with the single family home, owners are responsible for maintaining the property, the structures, and the land. Owners also pay their own mortgage, property taxes, and upkeep costs. The townhouse includes the same ownership rights and privileges as the traditional house, as well as joint ownership and maintenance obligations of common walls—sometimes called *party walls*—shared with neighboring structures that connect two or more townhouses. The land adjoining each townhouse can either be owned by the homeowner or by a homeowner or property owners association.

The Condominium Unit

Abraham Lincoln stated, "A house divided against itself cannot stand." Comedian Jackie Mason later quipped, "A house divided against itself is a condominium." Condominium, or *condo*, ownership consists of individual ownership of a space within a building and shared ownership of the common areas with the other unit owners. Unit owners have exclusive ownership and are entitled to possession of their respective units, but share ownership and use of common elements such as the lobby, elevators, rooftop, driveways, hallways, and landscaped areas. Although ancient in their roots, condominiums are a relatively modern legal invention created by U.S. state legislatures. So, while many of these state laws share common features, the exact details do differ from one state to another.

Condominiums are governed by a board of managers—a small group of owners responsible for overseeing the management of the building's daily operations. Whether the condominium is newly constructed or converted from a rental building, written documents govern the percentage of ownership of the building and the commonly held areas, as well as the residents' conduct with regard to the shared living arrangement.

Based on the percentage of ownership interest, a condominium owner must pay a monthly maintenance fee, often called *common charges*. Part of this payment goes toward the building's shared expenses, and the remainder is used to establish a reserve account. When a buyer is obtaining financing for a condominium unit, the lender will consider the monthly common charges when deciding how much to lend. Restrictions and rules applying to unit owners are usually less prohibitive in condominiums than in cooperatives. For example, the sale of the unit, subleasing, and financing are frequently heavily regulated in a cooperative apartment building. However, in a typical condominium, unit owners can freely sell and finance their units, as well as rent them, although some condominium communities do limit the right to rent. The recent trend for condominiums has been to increase regulation.

Condominiums come in all forms and may consist of a high-rise apartment building, a garden apartment complex, townhouses, attached houses, and even detached single-family homes. Amenities may include swimming pools, tennis courts, a clubhouse, hiking trails, and even a golf course. Although most condominiums do not require the extensive application process and interview that most cooperatives do, in some states condominium boards have the ability to exercise what is called a *right of first refusal*. The right of first refusal gives the building's board of managers the right to purchase or rent a condominium for the same price or rent—and under the same terms—as it is proposed to be sold or rented. For example, I once represented a television talk show host who had different political views than many of the existing residents of a particular condominium building. This celebrity attempted to buy a unit in the condo building, located on one of the most prestigious blocks in New York City, Central Park South. She got an accepted offer from the seller, signed the contract, and was thereafter told that she could not complete the purchase because the condominium's board had decided to exercise the right of first refusal and purchase the unit for itself. Because the condominium board decided to exercise the right of first refusal, my client—although accepted by the seller—could not buy the apartment she so desired.

The Cooperative Unit

The cooperative apartment, also known as a *co-op*, is a multi-unit building or building complex owned by a corporation that sells its shares to purchasers for an ownership interest in the whole arrangement, together with the exclusive right to lease an apartment in the building's premises. Entering into a proprietary lease with the cooperative corporation dictates that the cooperative residents—called *shareholders*—do not actually purchase the individual apartments. This ownership interest includes the right to use the common areas of the building as well as the exclusive right to possess a particular apartment. It may also include exclusive rights to an exterior living space, like a deck, patio, or terrace.

The number of shares allocated to each apartment is usually determined by the number of rooms, the location, and the size of each apartment, which is determined when the developer or the sponsor makes the initial offering as described in the offering plan. At closing, each shareholder is required to sign a proprietary lease, which defines the purchaser's rights and obligations in the cooperative corporation. At the same time, each shareholder also receives a stock certificate that indicates the number of ownership shares in the corporation. If the owner finances the deal, depending on the location, the owner may get only a copy of these documents to keep until the mortgage is paid off, whereupon he or she will then get the originals.

In addition to the proprietary lease, any bylaws, house rules, and amendments to each lease govern the rights and obligations of the cooperative corporation. Under these documents, cooperatives may impose ownership restrictions. Some of these might be rules governing the right of a shareholder to sublet or rent the unit, and the requirement that any sales, financing, or refinancing be formally approved by the corporation's board of directors. The rules and regulations may also deal with various building policies—whether pets are permitted, if residents can have a washing machine or dryer, or whether smoking is permitted in the apartments. Some common cooperative restrictions include rules regarding the percentage of uncarpeted floor space (cooperatives customarily require that 80 percent of floors be covered, excluding kitchens and baths), subletting the apartment, and noise constraints.

The board of directors, who are usually elected to one-, two-, or three-year terms by the shareholders,—govern the affairs of the corporation. One of their tasks is to establish the budget for the corporation's operations, which determines the monthly maintenance charges that each shareholder must pay. These charges are calculated by the number of shares owned, and this payment is referred to as the *maintenance*. The board allocates these funds to hire employees, pay its mortgage and real estate taxes, and to repair, clean, service, and manage the building. The board also appoints a managing agent to oversee the building's day-to-day affairs. This individual collects the maintenance charges, which are used to pay all the expenses of the cooperative corporation including mortgage, fuel, payroll, insurance, and taxes. The board may use its discretion to raise funds when necessary through a maintenance increase or a special assessment imposed on the shareholders. The board also determines the amount of money to be kept in the cooperative's reserve fund.

Most cooperative buildings have a mortgage on the building or complex, whose scheduled payments are made from the accumulated shareholder maintenance payments. If the cooperative cannot afford to make its mortgage payments as a result of shareholders' failure to pay their portion of the maintenance, the mortgage holder may foreclose the mortgage on the entire complex. While this rarely happens, it is not unheard of—and it would include all shareholders in the complex, regardless of whether some of them had been diligent in paying their maintenance payments to the cooperative. Condominiums and single family houses are free from such a common building mortgage, and therefore they may be more desirable in terms of financial security. However, all forms of homeownership have their share of advantages and disadvantages.

Although foreclosure is a possibility, it should be emphasized that there have been very few cases of foreclosed cooperative buildings since the Great Depression. However, this potential scenario does demonstrate the importance of buying into a cooperative corporation with a strong financial foundation. For this reason, I recommend that buyers have a real estate attorney and/or reputable accountant review the building's financial statements prior to signing the contract of sale.

Almost all cooperatives have a review and application process, which includes a complete financial and personal evaluation of the prospective purchaser. No matter how strong the applicant's financial situation, tax returns, proof of all assets and liabilities, and credit, employment, and reference checks appear to be, the board may still reject an applicant for any reason other than race, religion, sex, nationality, creed, and familial status. Furthermore, the board is not required to supply a reason for rejecting an applicant. Even persons as financially qualified as former President Richard Nixon have failed to pass a Manhattan cooperative board's review process. In most locations, the board's decision is final and almost immune from judicial challenge.

Many of these restrictions are intended to provide benefits to the existing owners. Cooperatives' exclusivity and approval process provide a mechanism to prohibit entrance by unsavory or even disagreeable characters, and to weed out applicants who do not meet minimum financial requirements. Some cooperative boards require a certain amount of liquid assets in the applicant's possession. These might include cash on hand and bank accounts along with monthly earnings demonstrating at least four times an applicant's monthly obligations, including loans, credit card debt, and any other financial obligations. This screening is meant to lessen the financial hazards discussed earlier and to bring the risk level of cooperative ownership more in line with that of owning a private home.

Despite the risks entailed, cooperatives also furnish many benefits. The staff employed by the cooperative provide for certain basic needs and chores. Former single-family homeowners can donate their lawn mowers and tools to another worthy homeowner, since the cooperative is required to maintain any grounds and to repair all major items inside your walls, common areas, and all major structural systems. Many cooperatives even provide repair services for minor repairs inside the apartments, such as fixing a washer or a faucet. In many cooperative doorman buildings, newspapers are delivered to your door, and services such as garbage collection, package storing, and dry cleaning may be included. In addition, some cooperatives provide services very similar to those of a hotel. Owners can leave the unit for long periods without worry or care—perfect for someone purchasing a cooperative unit as a pied-à-terre. And since the cooperatives are usually relatively dense housing, they're more likely to be nearer public transportation than a single family house would be.

Owning shares in a cooperative corporation also provides tax advantages similar to owning a single family home. Shareholders may deduct from their taxable income the percentage of payments made on the building's mortgage attributable to interest, as well as their portion of the real estate taxes paid by the cooperative corporation. This allows a shareholder three different income deductions: one for the building's mortgage interest, another for the shareholder's portion of the real estate taxes, and another for the shareholder's personal share loan. Such tax savings are exclusive to shareholders in qualifying cooperative apartments.

With all its restrictions and amenities, learning about cooperative ownership becomes essential before signing the contract to purchase.

Leonard H. Ritz, real estate attorney with Adam Leitman Bailey, P.C., shares his expertise:

Q. Why are condos more expensive than co-ops?

A. [RITZ:] I've never really accepted that co-ops sell cheaper than condos as gospel. There are too many unique factors involved in determining the price of real estate. But, assuming you found two absolutely identical apartments in two absolutely identical buildings that are operated in exactly the same manner, except that one is a condo and one is a co-op, here are four reasons that a condo would command a higher price:

Consider first the costs of ownership. Co-op maintenance payments and condo common charges pay for the costs of operating the building. As the buildings are identical, those costs will be identical, EXCEPT that co-op maintenance payments are going to be higher because they will also be increased by the apartment owners' share of real estate taxes on the building, and payments on the building's mortgage. So with a lower monthly charge, a buyer would be willing to pay more for a condo.

Consider next restrictions on transfer. In general, a co-op board has absolute control on approval of apartment sales, and a condo board has none. So it is generally easier and faster to buy and sell a condo apartment. This may increase the willingness of a condo purchaser to pay more. On the other hand, lack of control over who may be moving in next door to you can be seen as a detriment in some purchaser's view.

Next, consider risk of failure of your neighbors to pay their maintenance or common charges. In both buildings, either services will suffer or monthly costs will go up if there are significant arrears. But a co-op has an added risk: the risk of foreclosure on the building if taxes or the building mortgage are not paid. (In a condo, each owner pays their own taxes and mortgage, so no other apartment owner would be affected if someone fails to pay their own taxes or mortgage). All other things being equal, this added risk is a reason for co-op prices to be lower.

Finally, consider the ability to finance a purchase. Many co-ops prohibit financing; many that allow it limit it to 50–65 percent of the purchase price. Condos do not have such restrictions, so a purchaser can borrow 80 percent or more of the purchase price. A greater ability to obtain financing leads to higher prices.

FIGURE 4.1   Condos versus Co-Ops

The Condop

Real estate professionals tend to use two definitions of *condop*—the legal definition, and the definition everyone else uses. In the most common understanding of the term, a condop is defined as a cooperative building that follows the rules of a condominium. For example, such a building has a cooperative structure and ownership, but very limited regulation and restrictions on rentals and pets, and board approval would be nonexistent.

The legal definition of a condop is a building that is structured as a condominium with two units. The first unit consists of all of the commercial space, which is treated as a single legal chunk of space. That chunk may be divided into several stores, a laundry room, storage space, restaurants, or other commercial enterprises. Each enterprise is an ordinary tenant of the owner of the condominium unit. The other condominium unit in a condop consists of the entire block of apartments in the building treated as a single condominium unit, no matter how many apartments there are. However, this residential condominium unit is owned by a cooperative, which sells shares and gives out proprietary leases to each of the apartments in the residential block, thus running the residential side as a co-op within a condominium.

In other condop arrangements, the same corporation that owns the residential condominium unit also owns the commercial condominium unit.

MAKING THE DECISION

Once you have decided on the location and type of home that best suits you, it is time to choose the actual home to buy. Do *not* be impulsive; you ideally want to look at a minimum of ten different homes before reaching a final decision. Do not jump to make an offer on the first home you fall in love with. Be selective. If you are not sure whether to buy a co-op, condominium, or house, then look at several of each. What do you like and dislike about each? Compare and contrast the various types of housing to see which best satisfies your needs. Choose the type of property that is a good balance among the things you need, the things you would like to have, and the things you can afford.

CHAPTER SUMMARY AND INSIDER TIPS

- Check the building's financials, especially when purchasing a cooperative. It does not matter how beautiful the living room is if the building is heading for bankruptcy. Also check the owner occupancy rate of the building to ensure it meets financial institutions' requirements for financing.

- Compare cooperative and condominium units in similar buildings so that you can gain an understanding of the reasonable range for common charges/maintenance payments.

- Do not be convinced to purchase a cooperative unit based on a low maintenance payment alone. While this may be a significant advantage for an apartment to have, remember that this fee can increase at any time. Additionally, if a low maintenance payment puts the building's financials in jeopardy, this has the potential to ruin your investment. If the building's financials are not sound, be prepared for a tax called *an assessment*, which can be levied at any time to garner more income for the building.

- Check for additional fees or taxes for selling or leasing a unit. These may be costly and should be considered when purchasing.

- Check the comparables (prior sales in the building). Most buildings keep detailed records of sales transactions, which can be great indicators of a home's market value—especially when looking at recent transactions involving apartment types similar in size to the one that you are hoping to purchase.

- When buying into cooperatives, condominiums, or homeowner associations, check the rules to make sure they will accommodate your living requirements.

- When negotiating, ask the owners for the minimum price they would accept to close the deal. You may be pleasantly surprised by the answer and a deal may not be far off, especially if the property has been sitting on the market for a lengthy period of time.

- Some items are easier to negotiate than others. If both sides are stuck on the price, you can try asking the seller to throw in furniture at a certain price. For newly constructed condominiums, try asking the seller to pay any taxes involved in the transfer.

- Persuade with facts. But be sure that you do not insult the seller when negotiating the price, as you may lose the deal even if you are offering the highest price. When trying to negotiate a lower price, demonstrate
(continued)

(*continued*)

why it should be lower by showing how much it would cost to improve or repair the property. Avoid insulting the decor and the owner's taste.

- For cooperative purchases, your real estate broker and other persons in the cooperative building may be able to provide you with advice on that cooperative board's process. You should try to learn about the cooperative board and the type of people and financials that it tends to accept before signing the contract of sale and giving the down payment, since your down payment may be tied up for a couple of months or even longer while you await the board's decision.

Chapter 5 Conducting the Search

Finding Your Allies in the Real Estate Hunt

INSIDER TRADING—THE LEGAL WAY

While it is illegal to financially benefit from using inside information about a certain company's stock, in real estate obtaining information hidden from the general public's view is championed and celebrated, and many times it results in the most fantastic home deals.

As in building a house or fixing a fence, here too certain specific tools are best utilized to get the job done. In finding a home, information is the key to the real estate hunt. First, when looking for the best home within a predetermined price range, it is essential to have access to the widest array of homes for sale. Second, it is important to keep your ears attuned to the towns or cities in which potential homes are located in order to get important information about the community, schools, local events, and transportation systems, and to learn about the possibility of sanitation or nuclear plants coming to town, or that homes are being condemned as a result of defective construction.

MAKING FRIENDS IN STRANGE PLACES

Everyone and everything in the towns in which you're searching has the ability to provide potential insight into the home search. It is always worth spending time and money in local coffee shops and restaurants, and participating in other forms of local entertainment, in order to learn more about the neighborhood. You can even use window shopping as a means of seeing what kinds of people, goods, and services would become part of your home environment. Carefully observe the social dynamics.

People love to talk and be listened to, and most people are very generous with advice about their hometowns. To make the most of these opportunities, becoming a good interviewer is essential. Focus on big questions about the best and worst things about the town, as well as those that allow you to learn about the expertise of the person questioned—starting with "how long have you lived in this town?," should usually lead to a useful discussion.

Read the local newspapers and bulletin boards posted in stores to gain an understanding of the surroundings. If you are moving from a distant location, getting a hotel room for a weekend in the potential location will greatly aid in your attainment of information. Being friendly and dressing like the locals will make you seem approachable and breed respect, and these are therefore important considerations to factor into the search.

LOCATION, LOCATION, LOCATION

Traditionally, most people will narrow their home search according to location. In determining the best location, other factors besides price, proximity to work and to other family members, the beach, and the park should be considered in the selection criteria list. The following is a list of location-related factors that may or may not be important to your search but can too often be overlooked.

- Access to quality schools
- Safety of the surrounding area
- Local food
- Transportation
- Local entertainment
- Access to religious venues and quality of places of worship
- Access to medical facilities, doctors, and hospitals
- Commute to work
- Recreational facilities, such as a gym or swimming pool and parks
- Access and quality of public sewage and water systems
- Real estate taxes and fees assessed to a property or the town's citizens

Keep in mind that what one person might consider an asset another might view as a shortcoming. For example, a nearby pool or park could be seen as either convenient entertainment or a source of disturbing noise, whereas quality schools could be alluring for couples with children—or an unnecessary tax expense for those without.

DETERMINING FIXED MONTHLY AND YEARLY HOUSING COSTS

Because very few of us can make a wish list and find an affordable home with the entire list fulfilled, figuring out the most important criteria, as well as determining the difference in cost of living between one home and the next, will assist you in making the best choice out of your options. You would have already determined your home spending budget at the very beginning of the home buying process. An important factor in choosing one potential home over another will be seeing how the fixed monthly and yearly housing costs of each home fit within your budget.

For most Americans, this budget includes paying mortgage and real estate taxes. If you choose a fixed interest rate mortgage, this payment should not change for the life of the loan. However, real estate taxes may change depending on local taxes and policies. Besides learning about the applicable taxes, it is essential to look into the history of increases or decreases in past years and the stories behind these changes. For example, there's a law in New York City that limits the amount of increases in real estate taxes. In the early years of the new millennium, real estate taxes in New York City rose 18 percent. As a result, buyers could have known with relative certainty that any further increases in the short term would be unlikely or kept to a minimum. The sellers, real estate agents, the Internet, attorneys, and local tax collectors are all good sources for finding out about existing and past taxes paid on the home.

Another extremely important factor to consider with regard to taxes as well as numerous other quality of life issues is the presence or absence of one or a small number of large-scale employers. You will want to know whether any are supposed to come to town or are likely to be scaling back. There are many towns across the United States where land values have dropped as much as 80 percent in a single year due to the shutdown of a key employer. Your commute is another important pricing factor, since the cheaper home may be farther away from work or public transportation. The price of gas or the required use of a car and/or public transportation may then affect your budget. Check the cost of gas for the added mileage to one home versus other transportation costs for the home where you can walk to the train station or bus stop.

As your search continues and you explore all of these options, you should be able to narrow down potential home locations. Expect geographical areas to change based on pricing and other considerations, as well as the importance of your own individual housing needs.

MAKING A WISH LIST

You should make written lists that allow you to explore in detail your likes and dislikes over a period of time. These lists will assist you in making decisions; they will focus your search and save you valuable time. If there are going to be multiple persons residing in the home, no better means exists to get your spouse and family excited about moving than asking them to take part in the selection process. Encourage them to consider what must be included in your home and in its neighborhood, as well as what is desired and what would be terrific bonuses. The more time spent on narrowing down your location, desires, and price levels, the easier your search will be. This will save the real estate professional many hours of aimless exploration and will greatly shorten the process.

Of course, you may find your wish list constantly changing as you acquire information. Thus you will evolve from one simply jumping into the process to one who shops with a discerning eye.

REAL ESTATE BROKERS: THE GUARDIANS OF REAL ESTATE

For most of the nation, real estate brokers are the guardians of real estate sales. Many of the properties you visit will be represented by a real estate broker or an agent whom the seller has hired. A real estate agent whom you hire yourself to find a home for you is called a buyer's broker.

Real estate brokers and agents are experts at placing people in homes. The best of these professionals not only understand the make-up of neighborhoods, school districts, and communities in general, they also comprehend their clients' individual needs and concerns. This achieves the best match of home and buyer, and it saves buyers the hours it would otherwise take them to search for appropriate homes for sale. Instead, the professionals spend their own time searching and focusing their search on the buyer's greatest interests. Not only can brokers recognize and hone in on appropriate listings, but they also can provide access to listings as soon as they hit the market. These real estate professionals understand the different types of properties, the characteristics of a town, the idiosyncratic requirements of cooperative corporation boards, and the reputations of the local schools.

Real estate agents are territorial. They usually live near the homes they are selling and their listings are often limited to a relatively small area; as such, they can be great experts on their given area. However, a huge disparity exists between the best and a merely average real estate agent. As with any other life calling, the best professionals in the field are generally to be found in the most lucrative markets. Therefore, you should keep up your guard and be on the lookout for agents simply trying to fit you to a deal instead of looking for a deal that will fit you, particularly in less lucrative markets.

Since a large portion of the homes for sale are sold by real estate brokers, hiring a buyer's broker does not affect a home's sale price.

Unless contracted to do so, at no time would the buyer have to pay the buyer's broker. In almost all cases, the seller pays the broker's commission, customarily 5 or 6 percent, regardless of whether or not the commission has been divided between two brokers. Since the seller's broker will be paid more money in a *direct deal,* where the seller's broker does not have to share the commission with a buyer's broker, with all other things being equal, an agent may try to favor a potential buyer without a buyer's broker over one who has one, so that the agent does not have to split the commission. However, this strategy usually fails. The free market dictates and pushes prices, and this same broker has a duty and a priority to find the buyer with the highest price who can close on the deal. It is very rare that a bidding war will occur where the most financially capable buyer has the same prospects as another bidder who is not using a buyer's broker.

In any case, the benefits of having a buyer's broker generally outweigh the possibility that a bidding war will break out.

Attributes of the Best Buyer's Broker

If you have access to a great real estate professional, working with him or her will significantly increase your ability to find the best home for your money. However, only you can determine your own needs and wants, and only then will your broker be able to find the perfect glove to fit your hand. Within hours of a new home matching your criteria coming onto the market, your agent should be sending you the listing with commentary on the positive and negative points—and asking you if you want to see it.

Despite all of the advantages of the Internet, the real estate brokerage industry has managed to keep its own private databases of homes—often called the *Multiple Listing Service*—to itself. Ergo, a buyer's broker will usually have access to a listing before the public does.

A broker can track how long an older listing has been on the market and gauge whether the seller is being forced to sell quickly. The agent's analysis may also reveal why the home is not selling, or why it may be priced low. Reasons might include mold problems, noise from the train station across the street, or an oil tank that recently leaked in the backyard. In some cases, there may be no reason at all; it may simply be that the price just dropped and no buyer has yet taken advantage of the opportunity.

The buyer's broker also functions as your organizer and planner. He or she should be setting up appointments to see the properties and scheduling the greatest number of viewings within a limited amount of time to save the buyer countless hours of playing e-mail and telephone tag. Brokers should also use their expertise to discern those properties that may look worthy from the listing but do not actually fit your criteria.

The broker will also give you access to information on everything from taxes and local schools to pool club membership and even gossip. You can also look to this source for details on the history of any increases in a cooperative or condominium's carrying charges, locations of bike paths, and details about social events and local traditions.

Finding the Best Buyer's Broker

Just as the best looking person you see in a bar might not be your best choice in dating, the best broker for you is not necessarily the one who has smashed sales records. Someone who best understands and takes your needs into account will generally be both your best choice for a date and, as it turns out, your best choice for a broker as well.

A great place to start your search for a broker is to ask for referrals from others who have purchased in the neighborhoods you are considering.

Another approach to finding a buyer's broker is to attend open houses or make appointments to see properties to determine if you connect with an agent. Many brokers will not work with you if you are using several different agents, since the broker only gets paid if you do the deal with that agent. A wonderful way to find a match is to see brokers in action selling a property. This will allow you to gauge their knowledge base, see how good they are at connecting a buyer's needs to a property, and allow for a no-pressure interview to take place without the agent's knowledge. This is also a way to see if the agent has experience with the type of property you are looking for. You may find that the best broker in the town or city mostly sells two-million-dollar homes—so, if you have a budget of $200,000, you can assume the agent will not be particularly motivated to work with you. Ask such agents for additional referrals, and look up their sales success on the Internet. Many brokerages list their agents' sales history on their Web site.

You will frequently not be working with the referred agent but with one of his or her assistants. A remarkable number of these assistants or associate agents are hungrier than their bosses, and often they will have learned the best that their bosses have to offer. Still, you should be sure to interview any unknown broker before committing time and energy to the process. These mini-interviews provide you with a lot of free advice on homes in the area and the current market conditions.

Obviously, when home shopping, you do not want to risk being the agent's first customer. That agent will likely not have the skills and knowledge required to lead you past the land mines and into the best home for your money.

Additional Broker Considerations

You want to make sure that you and your broker's schedules coincide. If you can see properties only on certain days or during nights and weekends, you'll need your broker to have this time available for your meetings,—and also to put in the necessary hours searching for new listings.

Pay attention to how fast your agent replies to e-mails and calls you back. Don't hesitate to switch to someone else if you are not connecting to the agent or getting the attention you need. Just be aware that the broker that showed you the property first has a right to the commission, even if you see the home a second time with a different broker. You do not want a fight between brokers to kill your deal.

A Buyer's Broker's Kryptonite: FSBO (For Sale By Owner), and Searching Outside of Your Broker

A few listings exist that your broker will not have access to. Owners of For Sale By Owner (FSBO) homes may refuse to work with brokers to avoid having to pay their commission. Your broker certainly is not going to show you listings without being paid. So if you want to be extra diligent in your search, keep tabs of FSBO FOR SALE signs and check out these listings on your own.

Both sellers and their brokers advertise their properties where they can attract the most attention. This usually includes advertisements in the local newspaper, listings on the broker's Web site and, if applicable, a FOR SALE sign on the property or in a window. If you want to extend your search outside of your broker's range, it is essential for you to learn the places that local sellers advertise. This should never be your only means to find a suitable property, since you will lose out on access to many listings that are only in brokers' hands or may not have been advertised properly. Limited access to listings may hinder your search for a bargain. At the same time, you may find a great bargain in a FSBO sale. Because these properties are not so easily accessible, the restrictions on the market put buyers who do find the property at an advantage.

Looking for listings on your own in addition to using a broker will allow you to check whether your broker has been performing well or has missed any listings that interested you. In addition, sending the listings you find to your agent will reveal more to him or her about your likes and dislikes. However, be aware that in response to learning of your independent searches your broker may become outraged or even to threaten to quit.

MAXIMIZING THE SUCCESS OF THE SEARCH

Unless the market is very hot, hold off making an offer on a property until you are an expert on the local market within a few blocks or miles from your desired location. This means viewing many different properties that are possible candidates within your price range before making a final decision. These visits should be educational as you will be noting your likes and dislikes along the way, educating yourself and your broker on your tastes and needs.

Keep a written list of the contenders for your home purchase. On this list, take note of the possible benefits and disadvantages of the various properties and include applicable considerations, such as distance to public transportation and schools, on this list.

Bringing a camera becomes very useful—not only to remember the property and its unique quirks, but also to give you ideas of how you may want to decorate or improve your new home. In addition to taking photographs of the property, also take a picture of the property's address, even if just on a sheet of paper, so that you will remember which pictures relate to which property when you review them.

By taking your time to learn about different homes you may miss out on some potential homes, but it may be better to miss out on these opportunities than to take a chance and be stuck in a property that you regret buying for many years to come. Upon the first viewing, if you think you are really in love with a property, you will have to consider not only the obvious benefits but the definite risks of throwing caution to the wind. It is also a possibility that the properties you were interested in will still be on the market when you are ready to buy, and the prices may have even dropped by that time.

As soon as you have become educated on the market and narrowed down your choices, set up second showings. You will be amazed by how many new things you notice on a second visit. If you visited at night, conduct your second visit during the day, and vice versa. To garner extra insight, you may want to attempt to visit the home when the selling family is present. You may even be able to pick up on whether the seller would consider a reduced price for the home. I suggest bringing friends or relatives along for their different perspectives. Since this could be the biggest investment of your life, do not be afraid to ask questions and to make third and fourth appointments to see the home.

CHAPTER SUMMARY AND INSIDER TIPS

- You should create a home wish list over a period of time that will allow you to explore your desires, likes, and dislikes in detail. The more time you spend narrowing down your location, desires, and price levels, the easier your search will be. This list will also provide your broker with the ability to shorten the search and save many hours that could be spent looking at the wrong properties.

- In determining the best location, you should consider other factors in your criteria besides price, proximity to work, family, the beach, and the park. These elements may be local community crime rates, access to medical facilities, religious venues, and any other considerations that are applicable to your personal preferences.

- When looking for a buyer's broker, it is always good to start by asking for referrals from other people who have purchased in the neighborhoods you are considering. You may also want to inquire of those who know of a broker from someone else who recently purchased In the same area. Another approach to finding a buyer's broker is to attend open houses or make appointments to see properties and see if you find an agent with whom you can establish a good rapport.

- Many broker Web sites not only provide information about the real estate brokers but also list success stories, sometimes including each broker's closed transactions. This will allow you not only to see how effective your potential broker is in closing deals, but also where the broker has been successful.

- Everyone and everything in town can potentially provide you insight into the character of the town and neighborhood. It is always worth spending time and money in local coffee shops and restaurants, and participating in local events and entertainment to learn more about the area. Read the community newspapers and supermarket bulletin board postings to gain further understanding of the kind of place you are looking at.

- If you are contemplating moving from a substantial distance, it's worth booking a hotel room for a weekend in the area you are considering. This can serve both as a base of operations for your investigation and a source of information and informants in its own right. Hotel managers and desk clerks are usually only too happy to share insights and stories with you.

- Bring a camera along when viewing homes—not only to remember each property and its unique quirks, but also to give you ideas of how you may want to decorate or improve the place if you buy it. In addition to taking photographs of each property you are considering, also take a picture of the property's address so that you will remember which picture relates to which property when you review them.

- As soon as you have gotten to know the market better and narrowed down your choices, set up second showings. You will be amazed by how many new things you notice on a second visit. If you visited at night, the second visit should be during the day, and vice versa. Also bring friends or relatives along for their perspectives.

(continued)

(*continued*)

- An important factor in choosing one potential home over another will be seeing how the fixed monthly and yearly housing costs of each home fit within your budget. Real estate taxes may change depending on local taxes and policies. So besides learning about the applicable tax, it is essential to learn about the history of any increases or decreases in past years and the stories behind these changes.

- If you are not connecting with your buyer's broker or if you are not getting the attention you need, don't hesitate to switch to someone else. Just be aware that the broker that showed you the property first has a right to the commission, even if later you see the home a second time with a different broker. You do not want a fight between brokers to kill your deal.

- In addition to the properties you view with your broker, keep tabs of FSBO (For Sale By Owner) sale signs and check out these listings on your own. Look for advertisements in the local newspaper, listings on the broker's Web site, and even FOR SALE signs on properties or in windows.

Chapter 6 The Secret to Buying a Distressed Property

THE DNA OF A DEAL FINDER

Prospective homebuyers unintentionally pass up countless incredible deals. Recognizing an unusually good opportunity takes a trained, educated, and searching eye. Indeed, the best deals often don't even make it to the advertisement page. These deals go to the swift, inquisitive, and well equipped—almost never to the underprepared, unimaginative, and unsure.

Because distressed sellers need to sell as fast as possible to avoid foreclosure and other unaffordable costs, a deal maker's ready supply of cash is the king of distressed properties. However, uniquely prepared and competitive individuals can still compete at the negotiating table, even before they have used their acumen to accumulate surpluses of cash. These people have completed the necessary research on their personal home buying market well in advance, they know how much money to offer, and they may even have a bank ready to pull the trigger on a shaky mortgage.

Formal education and years of schooling usually do not play a factor in forming the deal. Recent studies have chipped away at the (incorrectly) widely held belief that the most influential Americans are graduates of the most influential institutions. An astonishing number of this power and money elite never even graduated from college, but what they lack in book knowledge they more than make up for in courage, frugality, ingenuity, intuition, and street smarts concerning the real estate market. The street is their university. This deal finder comes in all sorts of packages, many still donning their decade-old jeans and worn-out sneakers. Deal finders will often brag about their discovered treasures, but only after the deal is done and never during the hunt.

Many lessons learned by the deal finder can be applied to the one- or two-time home purchasers in search of that ever-elusive deal. Their common traits include in-depth knowledge of the real estate market, the courage to keep asking questions of good advisors, and the hunger to continue searching for the uncommon deal. Although luck can play a major role in any deal, most have found that the harder they try, the luckier they get.

DISTRESSED HOMES: THE MOST COMMON UNCOMMON DEALS

Besides uneducated or uninterested sellers, homeowners who are forced to sell quickly are among the best sources for deals. Although foreclosures can create a wonderful opportunity for a below market purchase price, an auction can force you to compete with many others, including professional investors and flippers. Bidding at auctions requires its own set of skills, not completely unrelated to playing poker. However, many of the best deals are to be found once the seller enters panic mode but before the gavel lands with the word sold.

FINDING THE UNCOMMON DEALS USING THE MOST COMMON MEANS

Deals are a lot like worms: You need to get your hands dirty to find the prize ones. You usually cannot see them until you do some digging, but as soon as you start, they'll begin to appear. You want to spread the word that you're looking for a home and would prefer a steal. Because a deal can come from just about anywhere, make sure as many people as possible learn about your quest, especially friends and family. The Internet has yet to conquer deal finding; good old gossip and information trading still provide the most common routes to uncommon deals. In fact, I regularly inquire about how buyers came across their great finds for every uncommon deal in which my companies have participated, and I almost always find out that the deals have stemmed from local information.

BECOMING A PROACTIVE DEAL HUNTER

Visit local real estate brokerages to make sure that they have you in mind for whenever a deal arises. While few agents specialize specifically in unusual deals, many brokerages have an agent or even a department that deals exclusively with foreclosures and other distressed sales.

When visiting homes, listen for any signals that indicate the home must be sold quickly. Simply asking whether the seller is in a hurry may be enough to provide your answer. When the sellers are in attendance at a showing, conversing with them can provide an excellent opportunity to learn whether there is a sense of time urgency in the sale. Additionally, when conducting the usual due diligence, speaking to town or city persons and the neighbors may also give you all kinds of useful inside information.

Many of my clients have proved industrious and creative in finding uncommon deals over the years. For instance, while I have had many clients join the board of directors of their condominium association for altruistic reasons, there have also been some who have joined for solely strategic purposes. Among other things, they wanted to learn when others in their building were in default of their regular payments. Owners who cannot keep up with monthly maintenance payments have a higher chance of defaulting on their mortgages. A strategically seated director might start by calling the owner to ask when payment would be made. Many times, this could be the root of a sale—and of course, a deal. It's also important to be tactful, of course, as intrusive questions could prompt the troubled owner to proclaim that the strategically seated director would be the very last person on earth to obtain the apartment.

When not on the board of directors or in a position of management, striking a more subtle approach, such as starting a casual conversation about anything besides the default, may be a safer or at least an easier tactic for your first attempt. However, no matter what the contents of the discussion, speaking to a person in financial distress will often lead to a door being slammed in your face.

I remember my frustration upon discovering that a member of the board of directors of a building where I owned a unit bought at least six distressed apartments for ridiculously low prices, which she then flipped or rented out. Although it seemed unfair to me that such access was not shared with the other unit owners, debatably, this board member's actions did not violate any laws or regulations—she simply used her uncommon knowledge to find uncommon deals.

CHAPTER SUMMARY AND INSIDER TIPS

- The best deals often don't even make it to the advertisement page. These deals go to the swift, inquisitive, and well equipped—almost never to the underprepared, unimaginative, and unsure.
- Most uncommon deals land in the hands of locals. Therefore, if you want to find one, become a transplant to the local community in question. Learn about the area where you want to buy and be willing to spend as much time as possible visiting properties on the market and meeting residents, brokers, neighbors, and government officials.
- Distressed deal finders have completed the necessary research on their personal home buying market well in advance, they know how much money to offer, and they may even have a bank ready to pull the trigger on a shaky mortgage.
- Deal finders' common traits include in-depth knowledge of the real estate market, the courage to keep asking questions of good advisors, and a hunger to continue searching for the uncommon deal.

- The Internet has yet to conquer deal finding; good old gossip and information trading still provide the most common routes to uncommon deals.

- In your distressed deal hunt, be proactive: Visit local real estate brokerages to make sure that they have you in mind for whenever a deal arises. When visiting homes, listen for any signals that indicate the home must be sold quickly. Simply asking whether the seller is in a hurry may be enough to provide your answer.

Chapter 7 Pre-Foreclosures and Short Sales

FINDING A PRE-FORECLOSURE

Many states' laws require legal proceedings for home foreclosures, but many others do not. The following information does not apply to states without judicial or court ordered foreclosures.

At the beginning of this kind of proceeding, the lender files a *notice of pendency* (otherwise known as a *lis pendens*) with the county clerk, court clerk, land records office, or registry. This document notifies all parties involved that a legal proceeding affecting a property's ownership interest has been initiated, and announces that a homeowner has defaulted on a mortgage and the foreclosure process has begun. The notice of pendency is useful to the deal hunter, as it potentially allows him or her to find a seller that may be forced to sell at a below-market price. These searches are not for the faint of heart. They provide the potential for an incredible deal for someone with specific information about a certain home or building, or who has been tracking a certain neighborhood and has a lot of free time.

However, these exhaustive searches can also be frustrating and often result in failure. Some typical obstacles include the inability to access the home, failing to discover that there is already a sale to another person in progress, finding that the home is heavily encumbered with liens, and encountering unusual difficulties in negotiation. Even if you're able to get past all of these, you may discover that the homeowners have either pulled out of your deal or have taken a better deal elsewhere, even after they have orally agreed to your terms.

Of course, finding a fantastic deal on one of the biggest investments of your lifetime will make the sweat, exhaustion, and the risks involved worthwhile.

Using the Internet to Find a Pre-Foreclosure

The Internet has arrived in the pre-foreclosure arena. Private for-profit Web sites provide lists of notice of pendency filings, many of which even offer free trial periods. I am aware of at least one Web site that provides dependable data. Since many real estate brokerages subscribe to these services, feel free to ask them about dependable resources in your area.

THE FORECLOSURE FILING

To find pending foreclosure cases, go to the county clerk's office, or your state's equivalent, for a list of the notice of pendency filings. Though these records are available to the public, they are almost never user-friendly. Once the computer, book, or list reaches your hands, you'll want to separate the cases initiated by banks, since those actions are most likely foreclosure filings.

Since the cases are usually indexed by plaintiff and defendant, you should be able to narrow the search considerably. First determine which banks are the most common lenders in the neighborhoods that interest you; then, simply look up those banks as plaintiffs in the land records index. For example, if Bank X is a typical mortgage bank in your area, going directly to Bank X listings is a lot faster than going through all the listings.

Next, you'll want to pull the actual cases related to the filings. Within minutes of reading the file you should be able to determine whether you have hooked a foreclosure case. The typical foreclosure action will ask for an amount owed by the owner as well as request the ownership of the property if such an amount has not been paid. At a minimum, the legal documents will include the owner's name, address, and the amount the lender seeks from the owner. It will even contain a copy of the mortgage and a number of the other documents signed by the owner at the time of purchase.

Another clue that the file you're reading is indeed a foreclosure case is that the case's name typically looks like the name of a bank against the name of one or two human beings, followed by several other defendants with names like John Doe #1. This combination—a bank's name as plaintiff and any Doe names—indicates that you are staring at a foreclosure case.

However, certain relevant details will usually not be contained in the legal documents. Some of these include the size of the home, the presence or absence of a pool in the backyard, the number of bedrooms, the number of bathrooms, and the finished or unfinished condition of the basement.

I call these searches *pre-foreclosure searches* because, in most states, a foreclosure only occurs upon the issuance of a judgment against the borrower where a court, sheriff, or marshal has ordered that the borrower no longer maintains legal ownership of the property. Depending on the state, the foreclosure process usually takes many months, even years, before completion. This provides plenty of time to complete a deal before a foreclosure auction conveys the property to its next owner.

In almost all states, a debtor can catch up on his mortgage payments even after the foreclosure process commences and, in some states, even after a judgment of foreclosure has been entered. The process of paying a delinquent mortgage after the foreclosure process has started is called a *reinstatement* of the mortgage. This is why it may still be beneficial to negotiate with a distressed seller even after a foreclosure action has commenced.

If you are already familiar with the property when searching for the case, and the property fits your needs, take the time to read that file. Most importantly, look for the history of the case. Has a foreclosure sale date been set? Is a court date pending where you may be able to meet the owner or appear at the next court date? Search as well for any written response by the owner; this could provide important clues to obtaining your dream home. In the states in which I have worked or visited, the personnel controlling these documents have always been helpful to people depending on the kindness of strangers. Many of them know as much as or even more about the foreclosure filings than the lawyers do.

It's important to know, however, that negotiating with the owner is futile once they've had possession of the property taken away from them. To that end, make sure the case is still pending before you leave the courthouse.

BUYING A SHORT SALE

When buying a home soon to be regarded as a short sale, the purchaser must recognize the new rules added to the home hunting game. Many times, this can result in an uncommon bargain.

What Is a Short Sale?

A short sale occurs when a lender agrees to take less than the amount owed on a loan from an owner. For a short sale to occur, the owner must persuade the lender that foreclosure would be inevitable without such a deal. It doesn't take much to convince a lender that a foreclosure would cost them, since this process usually moves slowly and involves a long period of time without any payment toward the property, not to mention substantial attorneys' fees. However, it's also necessary to convince the lender that they are unlikely to recoup the balance on the mortgage and associated fees from a property auction. Under those circumstances, the short sale benefits the lender. It allows the lender to receive a portion of its outstanding loan and lets the property turn over without significant delay. The lender still sustains a loss, but is cutting the losses by accepting the short sale.

Lenders do not seek out potential properties eligible for short sales. It takes a lot of paperwork, phone calls, and an overall aggressive pursuit on behalf of the owner to convince a busy bank to not only pay attention to this potential opportunity but to agree to take a loss on a loan pledged to the property and accept the seller as a hardship exception.

Ignoring the buyer's own needs for financing, there are three parties in short sales with usually conflicting goals. These are: the lender who currently holds a mortgage on the property; the property's owner; and the buyer. The lender — who has issued the loan assuming that it would make a profit and so will not relish sustaining a loss—will look to make that loss as small as possible. The owner who owes the bank that money probably has not fully accepted the idea of losing the home, and may actually have very little interest in the short sale's price. This is a person who may be so depressed by the entire transaction as to become totally uncooperative. The purchaser is a bargain hunter who may have to show some sensitivity to the seller's situation in order to get anything accomplished and obviously has a set of goals completely at odds with those of both the lender and the seller.

For bargain hunting buyers, the short sale experience can delay a deal for many months as the lender seems to tease the seller as to whether it will accept the seller's price and write off the rest of the loan. Therefore, make sure that you have a binding contract with the seller before you pour hours into the process.

I recommend that savvy buyers try to get not-so-communicative sellers to join together with them to push the process forward. Lenders will not speak to a potential buyer without written permission from the seller, but lenders will allow joint phone calls. Many times, phone calls to the proper person can take your short sale straight to the top of the pile. Additionally, making sure you get to see the seller's application and seeing that it has provided all of the required paperwork can help push the process forward.

You may be able to use your familiarity with the short sale process to motivate a seller to lower the price. By the time the words short sale are in most sellers' vocabulary, they are usually resigned to the fact that they are not going to make a profit on the home. Instead, their chief goal at this point is to avoid having to make payments on a mortgage after no longer owning the home. Once you are familiar with the short sale process, you can offer your services in getting the lender to accept a lower price in exchange for a bargain on the sales price and convince the seller that it is in both your interests.

The buyer is also racing against the clock in many short sales, as the lender may have filed for foreclosure. It is critical in all of these situations to determine whether the seller has clear title to the property, or if title is about to be taken away. You do not want to waste your efforts entering into a contract and working toward a sale only to find out that the home has already been auctioned off to someone else.

You also want to avoid making the home sale contingent upon a short sale. Instead, you want to have a secure price for the property and to make sure the contract allows you to force a sale even if the short sale fails to occur.

LEARNING MORE ABOUT THE DISTRESSED PROPERTY

When you are doing a blind search, before reading the entire file, take down the basic information and make sure the case is not winding down before plunging into action. To determine whether this property meets your criteria, start with an Internet search using the property's address, since this may reveal that the property is listed with a broker or provide other useful information. Also, walk or drive past the potential home.

If the property has a doorman, security guard, or any other employee, you can ask about the line of apartments applicable to the unit to determine its suitability. For example, ask how many bedrooms the K line of apartments contains. You may even be able to get your hands on a floor plan at a real estate brokerage's office. For single family homes, remember that stepping onto someone else's property may constitute illegal trespassing, so view the house from as close as possible while keeping the required distance. While walking on a sidewalk directly parallel to the front door may be perfectly acceptable, it is generally a bad idea to enter the property through a gate.

MAKING CONTACT WITH A DISTRESSED OWNER

Although it's not as terrible as discussing impending divorce or recent job loss, attempting to engage complete strangers in chats about their precarious financial situations certainly falls under the category of unpleasant conversations.

To acquire the trust of the distressed owner, start by dressing appropriately. First impressions matter, so always dress conservatively. You will be approaching someone in a difficult financial spot. So be sensitive—you do not want to appear too slick or even rich. Forego the jewelry unless it is a wedding ring or conservative earrings. Concerning the suit, you may want to skip the tie depending on the situation, and tight or ripped jeans and sweatpants are always out. Dress for this meeting like you are going to an interview. You may find that approaching a distressed owner is in fact a very similar experience to a daunting job interview, and perhaps even more difficult.

Start the conversation by introducing yourself and letting the owner know your home buying intentions. Ask the distressed owner about whether anyone is selling homes in the area or may be soon putting a property on the market. If that does not yield any results, you may want to mention that you are interested in the area and ask for general advice or any information that the distressed owner is willing to share. Hopefully you will be informed that the home in question is for sale and be invited inside as a guest. If the owner does not bite or take the hint, reveal the information you have gathered on the property in question and discuss the advantages of selling the property to you instead of waiting for the foreclosure to take place.

Once you reveal that you are aware of the foreclosure action, the conversation may end abruptly. Win or lose, always leave your cell phone number with the distressed owner, as you never know when an owner's attitude about selling the home will change.

Negotiating a Deal with the Distressed Owner

When the distressed owner agrees to listen to you, make the most of this opportunity. Many distressed owners do not know the benefits of avoiding a foreclosure. You can point out that in selling the home to you they will avoid having to pay court costs as well as other charges pertaining to the foreclosure sale, and that any foreclosure auction will likely sell the property at the lowest possible price, certainly less than you are prepared to offer. Share this with them and they may treat you as a savior if you can deliver the results promised.

Remember the two points crucial to the discussion: time and money. It may put you in an advantageous position to explain to the distressed owner that once you agree upon a sale price you are not in a rush and can wait three or six months or even longer before taking possession. Offer these months at no charge to further convince the owner. Make this offer as soon as the negotiating begins.

Explain that, without charge, you will assist in contacting the bank and stopping the foreclosure. Of course, the bank will not speak with you without oral or even written permission from the owner, and it may be best for the two of you to make the first call on the bank together.

You should also bring to the distressed owner's attention how a foreclosure may prohibit the owner from buying another property for many years to come, whereas a sale to you could keep the owner financially credible. Make the distressed owner aware that both of your interests are aligned—that a sale to you fulfils the goals of avoiding foreclosure and even bankruptcy, lessening the damage done to the owner's credit, and could even put more money into the owner's pocket.

Educating and Learning from the Distressed Owner

If you have not been kicked out of the home and you are working on negotiating a deal, make sure that you carefully listen to the distressed owner. Remember, this person has needs and desires too. Also, the distressed owner may have misconceptions and questions that will need answering before closing the deal. If you lose the trust of the distressed owner, you will most likely kill the deal. Many times, the distressed owner will want to discuss what caused the situation. The empathy that you demonstrate can go a long way. Any information gained will also assist you in deciding how to proceed with the deal. For instance, if you hear the word divorce mentioned in the conversation, this may put you on guard, since you may find that you are able to make a deal with one spouse but the other refuses to participate. Both husband and wife may have property rights to the home, or you may even find that the home cannot be sold until the divorce is final.

Once you've established your credibility, ask for any documents that the distressed owner has received from the bank or lawyers. Discuss whether the home has one loan or mortgage or more, and learn the amounts of each. Hopefully, the owner will know and share this information with you, and let you know about other liens and debts tied to the property along with any problems with the home's physical condition. Ask about the upkeep of the house and whether it has been expensive. Such a question may lead to important information about a leak in the basement or potential roof repair.

Once a Deal Has Been Negotiated

You should be proud of yourself once you come to terms with the distressed owner; however, you still have a lot of work to do. Remember — you're dealing with someone who must sell his or her home, and you have the unique opportunity to make this purchase at a discount without competing with other potential buyers. Use this to your advantage throughout the lengthy process.

Start with a lien and judgment search on the property to determine the actual amounts due to the bank and other creditors. You may find that these amounts are too cumbersome, which may kill the deal on the spot. Or you may decide to contact the bank along with the owner to work on closing the deal. Once you are serious about closing the deal, send in an inspector or engineer to check the physical condition of the home, just as I describe in this book, but in this case do not expect the seller to fork out money for repairs or renovations.

The Contract of Sale

Assuming that the terms to which you and the buyer have agreed still work after learning about the debts that need to be paid off at closing, put the terms agreed upon into a contract of sale.

Remember that although this person may be someone who is nice to meet for coffee, he or she is essentially judgment-proof at the moment. Therefore, attempt to put down as little money as possible as a down payment. Keep this money with your attorney or expect never to see it again. Make sure the contract of sale allows you to walk away from the deal if you cannot get a mortgage on the property as a result of unexpected debts that need to be paid off. Make sure that the closing does not take place until the home is empty; alternatively, make sure you have a post-possession agreement allowing you to evict the occupants in case they do not vacate by the agreed upon time.

MY STORY: MY UNCOMMON DEAL

A little bit of luck can make or break the uncommon deal. In one of my own real estate adventures, this luck—and some serious due diligence— ended up saving the day.

I had made very clear to everyone I knew that I was on the market to buy another home—but only "if it was a steal," as I repeated many times. One of the persons with whom I shared this information was another resident in my building, Debbie, who lived two floors below me. We had become friends after spending time together sharing our daily exploits. One night after work, she came to my apartment and reported that the elderly lady who lived in an apartment on her floor had died the night before, and that yellow police tape now blocked her apartment doors.

In life, death is generally mourned as a great loss. However, in real estate, death is frequently—for the lack of a better word—celebrated. The deceased tenant who previously lived in the unit had a special status that restricted the amount that could be charged for rent. Upon the termination of her tenancy, the apartment could be rented or sold for whatever the market could bear.

After learning more about the situation, I immediately sought to determine who owned the apartment and how to find him. Since the Internet was not widely used at this time, I was forced to rely on old-fashioned methods like asking building employees and neighbors. Within a few minutes of speaking with the doorman, I learned that the superintendent had previously completed work for the owner, who actually also owned several other units in the building. Not only did I then contact the superintendent; I also offered him payment if he assisted me in securing the apartment.

This effort proved to pay off better than I could have imagined. I was able to reach the owner, and he invited me into his plush condominium a few blocks away. He was very charming, and keen to share his history with the building and talk about his life in general. Although I listened intently, I did not forget why I was there; I had come to negotiate.

Before my visit, I had already contacted the building manager and obtained information on all of the building's sales since its construction. Focusing particularly on recently sold units in the line where the apartment in question resided, I learned how similar apartments sold in the building. Asking the superintendent to determine how much it would cost to put the apartment in habitable condition and inspecting the apartment myself through the super's set of keys proved invaluable opportunities, especially since the apartment had been secured from the public.

As expected, the apartment's owner called the superintendent to determine its condition. To this day, I'm still not sure whether my payment, along with my promise to pay him even more money if I secured the unit, affected the super's response. However, since I was a decent provider to the building's staff at Christmas time, the super had every reason to trust that I was good for my word.

During my detective research, I realized that I had stepped on gold. The unit in question had *unsold shares*—a special ownership status meaning that an owner purchasing as an investor would inherit special rights. These special rights meant that the qualifying purchaser would not have to follow many of the building's restrictions on subletting, or to pay any fees concerning subletting the apartment. To qualify, the seller had to have purchased the unit directly from the developer who converted the building to cooperative housing and to have never moved into the unit— and this, fortunately, was the case.

Inside the owner's apartment, Debbie and I quickly learned that he loved to talk, and he had the most amazing stories. I remember thinking that I could learn a lot from this man. Getting the owner to make the first offer had been my initial goal, but I failed. He eventually asked me how much I wanted to pay.

"So how much do you want to buy the place for?"

"I'm not sure," I replied. "I like the building, but this unit is a wreck and needs a total rehabilitation. But I am still very interested in buying it."

"You seem like a very nice gentleman. You and your friend make a nice couple."

(*continued*)

(*continued*)

I didn't interrupt the owner to tell him that we were just friends—and that if I hadn't been smart enough to keep the relationship strictly platonic, I probably wouldn't have been sitting there at that moment.

"I have done many deals in my life, and helped many a couple purchase their homes," he continued, "and I have always been fair."

"I'm glad to hear that. Your unit is a little bit bigger than mine, but it needs a lot more work. In fact, my unit was in pristine condition when I bought it, and I paid $70,000 two years ago. Do you think that would be a fair offer?"

I was a bit surprised that the owner didn't mention the deceased at all during our entire exchange, especially since she had been his tenant for decades. Instead, he peppered me with questions and, as the negotiation continued, I learned that he really had no idea how to value the unit. It started to seem that he did not care very much about finding out its market value. We settled on a price of $90,000, despite the fact that he could have gotten $250,000 easily—not including the $10,000 needed for renovations. Indeed, similar units sold for $450,000 about a decade later.

Just when I thought the hard part was over, I learned that this roller coaster of a deal had only just begun. Shortly after signing the contract of sale, I found out that the owner was actually a fraud. He'd been prosecuted by the United States Attorney's Office for stealing and for failing to pay taxes to the federal government. At the time we signed the contract of sale, he owed millions in taxes to the federal government.

However, two weeks prior, I had made one of the luckiest business decisions of my life. When negotiating the contract of sale, I crossed out a provision where the buyer—me—became responsible for paying any liens above $2,500. Without deleting this provision, he would have argued that I had to pay the debt owed on the unit to the Internal Revenue Service, instead of him.

I soon came to realize that this man had never intended to sell me the unit. Keeping my down payment of 10 percent of the purchase price was actually his objective. However, I also knew that I had secured an incredible deal—and I was not letting this prize bull out of my hands without a battle.

I ran a search on the property during which I found out about the owner's debt to the IRS. I called and negotiated with the government until I had confirmation that they would in fact approve the sale and collect the proceeds at the closing. Instead of the balance of the payment going to the seller, the IRS picked up the money at the closing in exchange for a receipt lessening the debt the seller owed the government by the amount paid.

Four important factors were key to my securing this uncommon deal. First, there was my negotiation of an extremely below-market price for an apartment. Brevity had been the key to this success. By moving quickly in collecting information and negotiating a price, I curbed the seller's motivation to find out what the unit could sell for on the free market. Of course, his problems with the law assisted in limiting his motivation to obtain the highest possible price.

Second, I properly protected myself at the contract stage by not only deleting the paragraph that had me paying his debt, but also by insisting in the contract of sale that upon the owner's refusal to sell the unit, I could ask a judge to order that I receive the keys.

Third, I convinced the IRS to approve the deal without having to provide an appraisal that could have led to the IRS asking for more money.

Finally, my irrepressible behavior demonstrated to the owner that I would not quit, even if that meant going to court to close the deal instead of walking away from my money.

A combination of luck, good detective work, and sweat got this uncommon deal done. Twelve years later, I still own the unit and as a result of having two really great tenants, the place looks immaculate and provides a nice home.

CHAPTER SUMMARY AND INSIDER TIPS

- Understanding the current status of a foreclosure court action does not require a legal degree, but you will most likely feel like you need one. Ask for assistance from the court personnel, and be ready to send thank you letters to their bosses for their assistance. Not only will you make friends forever, but you will also have assistance every time you walk into the courthouse.

- When contemplating whether to buy a short sale, make sure that you have a binding contract with the seller before devoting hours of your time to the process. You also want to avoid making the home sale contingent upon a short sale. Instead, you want a secure price for the property and to make sure the contract allows you to force a sale even if the short sale fails to occur.

- Persuade the seller to join forces with you for optimal results in a short sale. Make calls on the seller's behalf, speak to the lender together, and review the seller's application to make sure that the seller submits all

(*continued*)

(continued)

required paperwork. Pushing the short sale forward works in your favor and may put you in a better position to secure a bargain purchase price on the property.

- Utilize the services of a qualified engineer before signing the contract, or make sure the contract gives you the opportunity to pull out if major repairs make the deal much less of a bargain. The engineer should determine whether the home needs significant repairs that will cost the difference between an uncommon below-market deal and an uncommonly bad one. Especially with distressed sales, remember that you are buying the home in *as is* condition. So any problems with the structure are built into the price; do not expect to obtain a further discount in the purchase price from the seller at closing.

- Attempt to put down as little money as possible as a down payment and to keep the down payment deposited with your attorney. Given your seller's financial distress, you may never see your money again. Make sure the contract of sale allows you to walk away from the deal if you cannot get a mortgage on the property because the debt liens on the property overwhelm its value. Another reason that distressed sales are particularly risky is that many times sellers, not wanting to leave their homes behind, take drastic measures to stay in them as long as possible.

- Try not to hand over the purchase price until the home is vacant and ready for you to take possession. Even if you need to delay the closing for months, such a wait may ultimately save you from having to start an eviction action or from the seller trying to undo the sale and keep your money in a legal action. By delaying the closing until complete vacancy if possible, you can avoid unnecessary legal fees. Even the best post-possession agreement may force legal action to be commenced.

- When agreeing to a post-possession agreement, retain a qualified attorney or intermediary to bulletproof the document so you can ensure that the seller really does vacate on the date indicated in the agreement.

- When purchasing a multi-family dwelling with existing tenants, make sure that any lease agreements have been disclosed and the rights to the tenancies are transferred to you upon your purchase. This should include a record of monies owed to the seller, transfer to you of any security deposited with the owner, and allocation of responsibilities for utilities and property usage.

Chapter 8 Foreclosures and Bank-Owned Properties

FINDING A FORECLOSURE SALE

Foreclosure notices are typically posted at courthouses, clerk's offices, town halls, and printed in newspapers. They list the property's address, the date, time, and place when the bidding will occur and, sometimes, other relevant information such as the minimum acceptable bid, which is usually the amount owed on the mortgage loan. Though the location of the auction varies widely depending upon the state in which the property is located, bidders will frequently meet at the entrance to the property itself, or on the courthouse steps, or be directed to a room somewhere else. I have seen foreclosure sales with crowds standing in the room at convention sites, and others with only two or three people in attendance. While gavels are traditional in some places, in no state does the law require them.

BUYING A FORECLOSED PROPERTY

At the time you are attending a foreclosure auction, the foreclosure litigation should be concluded, along with the removal of all liens, encumbrances, and judgments previously affecting the buyer's ability to obtain clear title to the property. But although the foreclosure sale is supposed to extinguish all outstanding liens, this is not always the case.

First, you want to make sure that the foreclosing party has the most senior lien because, if it does not, your purchase at foreclosure may be swallowed into the larger lien. Running a title or lien search on the property will identify the foreclosing lien's seniority position. If the foreclosing lien is second or third, and the older liens have not expired due to the statute of limitations or for any other reason, then the purchaser would have to foreclose or pay off the older liens to obtain clear title.

Second, any lien or encumbrance not named in the foreclosure action may force the foreclosure sale to be overturned. The title or lien search should allow you to identify such liens. I strongly suggest that you do not enter the foreclosure world without the guidance of a professional.

ATTENDING THE FORECLOSURE AUCTION

A foreclosure auction is not the time to tell everyone how much you love or know about the property. It is not a sharing time or an occasion to tell other people about the greatest features of the home. It is the time to ask a lot of questions and to learn as much as possible from everyone else while surrendering no information of your own. Many auctions will have individuals in attendance who frequent these auctions as a profession. In some cases, only sparse details about the home will be available, and people will bid based only on limited information, such as details from a foreclosure Internet service that provides basic data like taxes, the amount of the mortgage, and sales history. Get to the auction extra early to familiarize yourself with the protocol and to make sure you have time to properly register and get to the right place.

DETERMINING HOW MUCH MONEY TO BRING TO THE AUCTION

It is not only how *much* money you bring to the foreclosure sales, but also *how* you bring the money. The auctioneer will usually require between 5 and 10 percent of the auction price as a down payment upon obtaining the winning bid, or even just to register for the auction. You do not want to overpay and certainly do not want to underpay. Most auctions require bank checks or certified funds as payment. Depending on the approximate purchase price, you will want to bring very small increments of payment. For example, if the property range is around $100,000 and you need to deposit 10 percent at the auction, bring five $1,000 checks and ten checks of $500.

FORECLOSURE PITFALLS: TAKING THE PROPERTY *AS IS* AND EVICTING THE OCCUPANTS

The auction usually ends within a few minutes; if you are the winning bidder, you would have just bought a home in as is condition. You will not have any time after the auction to negotiate a credit for repairs, and you may be forced to evict the occupants in possession as well as deal with the issues of having to do serious rehabilitation to the property.

LOSING THE PROPERTY TO REDEMPTION LAWS

In a number of states, the foreclosure auction is not necessarily the end of the story. In these states, under some circumstances, the one who defaulted on payments may have the opportunity to reimburse you for the money you laid out at the auction in order to reacquire title to the property. These laws, where they exist, specify timing and amounts and typically do not include ancillary expenses you may have associated with the purchase you thought you made.

FINANCING THE PURCHASE

The lender may also give you very short and strict terms to complete the purchase. Many foreclosure sales require you to pay the balance within 30 to 60 days, on pain of the buyer losing the down payment made at the auction. Although many traditional buyers can obtain a loan from the foreclosing bank or complete the deal with a third bank in time, the terms of the sale do not usually allow for adjournments or other typical delays when financing a home. Therefore, purchasing at foreclosure is for neither the faint of heart nor the financially uncertain.

Generally, when the foreclosure concerns a cooperative unit, the cooperative will not be required to accept your purchase just because you are the winning bidder. The winning bidder may have to place the unit back on the market if the board fails to approve the person who purchased the home.

REO/BANK-OWNED PROPERTIES

Most of the pitfalls discussed in relation to foreclosures do not affect bank-owned property sales, often referred to as REOs (Real Estate Owned). These properties are usually homes kept by the banks, often because they failed to receive an adequate outside bid at foreclosure and so the bank basically pulls it off the foreclosure shelf. Or, the bank may have received the property when the owner, feeling a foreclosure was imminent, offered to deed the property over to the bank instead and the bank saw its best interest in accepting that offer.

Because the deed is in the bank's name already, a buyer can be reasonably confident that no ghosts or liens will come out from hiding to tie the property up in litigation or affect the prospective buyer's ability to own the home outright.

I have seen some of the most uncommon deals come from bank-owned properties. The reason usually comes from the fact that banks are in the business of loaning money and not maintaining and owning real estate. Properties kept on their balance sheets show negatively on the bank executive's report. So, the bank is usually eager to unload them quickly, often at a discount. Banks also do not want to pay the upkeep and taxes on foreclosed properties.

Although historically bank-owned property deals were great bargains, in many locations they are no longer as good as they used to be. More and more banks use outside real estate brokers to sell these properties instead of selling them in-house. Because of the more aggressive manner in which brokers find buyers, the prices often mirror the free market instead of the reduced prices usually associated with distressed properties. Nevertheless, I still come across individuals who either had a friend at a bank or who proactively contacted banks themselves and came away with a wonderful home or investment as a result.

Making bank-owned properties a part of your home search could prove fruitful if you are willing to spend the time and energy to hunt down these deals.

MY STORY: A FORECLOSURE SALE AND PURCHASE

To explain why I was sent into the auction room to bust a foreclosure sale, I need to start from the middle of the story.

John, Drew, and Frank each owned a one-third interest in a condominium unit. After two costly divorces and a number of bad investments, John owed a lot of money to a lot of people. One of these creditors, Bill, had a large judgment against John and decided to collect it from John's only substantial investment— the one-third interest in the condo. The last thing John's partners wanted was a stranger butting into their partnership, getting in the way of the condo's lucrative rental income. Since it was a foregone conclusion that John would lose his financial interest in the property, his brother intended to buy John's share.

For almost three years after being retained as John's attorney, I had so far managed to frustrate Bill's attempts to foreclose on the property. But since the judge had set the final date for the foreclosure sale, D-Day was just around the corner.

I knew there was a substantial danger that there would be bidders at the auction who had not done their homework and had not found out that they would be buying into a partnership with two other partners, rather than being able to run the property themselves. So, I went to the auction to explain the deal to the bidders and to persuade them to forego the deal.

Thankfully, the property had not been advertised properly and only eight potential bidders showed up. I got to the auction early and showed those present a lien search detailing the handicaps on the property. I also described how heavily this deal had been litigated and what a headache

(continued)

(continued)

the property would be for any third party purchaser. I made sure to keep a close eye on the auctioneer who remained very calm and stoic. Failing to cut me off, I was able to give a speech explaining the history of the property and its litigation.

As soon as I finished expressing to the bidders how bad becoming a partner on the property would be, the auction began and almost immediately ended. No one had bid the auction's minimum and I assumed that I had saved the day. I walked out of the foreclosure auction almost skipping with enthusiasm.

My excitement quickly faded the next day, however, as I discovered that Bill was about to sell his interest to a fourth party on his own, meaning that Drew and Frank would soon have a new partner. Fortunately however, the sale fell through and Bill failed to shift the unit to a new partner. Since Drew and Frank now wanted to sell the property and remained the property's only owners, I recommended an up-and-coming broker, named James Famularo, to sell the property. James did his job and did it well—he found a buyer, the publisher of a newly founded magazine.

At the closing, everyone made out very well. Each of the remaining partners, who had originally purchased the property for about $50,000 each, wound up getting nearly $400,000 at closing. Bill's judgment got paid off at closing.

As it turned out, if there had been a winning bidder at the foreclosure auction, that winning bid would have netted a profit of some $160,000 a few months later. So, although the unknowns were great, taking the risk of buying the property at foreclosure for the minimum price could have netted the winner a quick 67 percent profit on the investment.

CHAPTER SUMMARY AND INSIDER TIPS

- When considering purchasing a home at a foreclosure sale, remember that although the sale usually extinguishes all outstanding liens, this is not always the case. This is why it's so important to conduct a title or lien search, which would allow you to identify any liens, during a foreclosure purchase. Because of the risk involved, I strongly suggest that you do not enter the foreclosure world without professional guidance.
- When bidding to purchase a home at a foreclosure sale, make sure that the foreclosing party has the most senior lien, since if they do not, your

purchase at foreclosure may be swallowed into the larger lien and you may have to foreclose or pay off the older liens to obtain clear title.

- Arrive at the foreclosure auction extra early in order to get properly set up. Ask and learn a lot; volunteer nothing.

- At a foreclosure auction, the auctioneer will usually require between 5 and 10 percent of the auction price as a down payment upon obtaining the winning bid or even just to register for the auction.

- Take small increments of certified checks or bank funds to the auction for payment. For example, if the property range is around $100,000 and you will need to deposit 10 percent at the auction, bring five $1,000 checks and ten $500 checks.

- Many states have redemption laws that provide a certain amount of time for the original owner to buy the property back at the mortgage price amount plus legal and bank fees. You may want to check on the procedure in your state before pouring hours of your time and energy into a purchase that you may never obtain.

- Bank-owned properties are generally a safer bet than foreclosures. Title is generally clear and there are no redemption laws to worry about. Since the deed is in the bank's name already, a buyer can be confident that no ghosts or liens will come out from hiding to tie the property up in litigation or affect the prospective buyer's ability to own the home outright.

- Bidding at auctions requires its own set of skills, not completely unrelated to playing poker. However, many of the best deals are to be found once the seller enters panic mode but before the gavel lands with the word "sold."

Chapter 9 Hidden Land Mines to Look Out for

Although most real estate transactions result in a rewarding experience, a costly problem or misunderstanding can occasionally hit a buyer like a Category 5 hurricane. You can prevent most of these storms or surprises with a little bit of information, which should help you recognize a potential problem before closing on the purchase. This chapter presents some of the most common hidden dangers and surprises that I have encountered during my career in real estate.

DETERMINE WHETHER THE HOME IS LEGALLY HABITABLE

Governments regulate housing in the name of safety. In order to earn permissible occupancy rights, homes must comply with housing regulations that dictate a home's size, number of bedrooms and occupants, purpose of use, and ensure compliance with other building and safety standards. Some locations require that residents obtain a document (usually called a *certificate of occupancy*) from the municipality where the home is to be located before they are actually allowed to live in it. In most cases, when purchasing a property, your real estate professional runs a search for documents ensuring legal compliance with these laws. Payment for the home should not be made until a verdict has been obtained that the home has been built safely and in compliance with the government's regulations.

In a very few cases, homes fail these tests for having been built contrary to permitted building standards. One particular situation that I encountered involved a builder who had constructed the home two stories higher than the local law allowed. Because of this improper building, the purchasers lived for years under the threat of eviction by the city government. As a result, the property lacked monetary value, was unattractive to buyers, and could not obtain lender financing.

In another instance, the purchasers discovered that the three-bedroom apartment they had purchased was actually a one-bedroom apartment with two storage spaces, due to the fact that their unit's windows were directly on the border with the adjacent property. If the next door neighbor developed his land with a building going right to that same border, two of the supposed bedrooms would have windows that looked out on nothing but bricks, mere inches away. Under state law, this potential lack of a view made these supposed bedrooms ineligible for such use, and reduced them to the status of very large closets. So the apartment would have to be marketed as a one-bedroom instead of as a three when this buyer tried to sell—which would, of course, vastly reduce its resale value.

Although the government does not generally prosecute persons for living in rooms without windows, no dwelling should be purchased without proper knowledge of whether it complies with the law.

BE AWARE OF THE NUMBER OF UNITS SOLD AND OCCUPIED IN NEWLY CONSTRUCTED APARTMENT DEVELOPMENTS

When considering purchasing a home in a newly constructed apartment development, be aware that lenders may refuse to loan money to purchasers until after the sponsor has sold a certain number of units. Many traditional lenders require that between 50 and 70 percent of units be in contract or sold before they will provide lender financing. Without lender financing, not only will many purchasers be unable to buy into the development, but the lack of available financing channels can damage the development's financial integrity. The sponsor's inability to sell units can deprive the development of the resources it needs to pay for utilities, trash disposal, and other necessities like repairs.

This same analysis applies to any development where a large number of vacancies exist, whether due to lack of sales or foreclosures. In many of these situations, such developments' units eventually get sold off at lower prices or turned into rental units.

CLEAR ALL LIENS AND OBTAIN SIGNOFFS FOR EXTENSIONS AND ALTERATIONS BEFORE CLOSING ON A HOME

Since most homes are purchased in as is condition, the seller is not usually liable to a buyer for any messes—physical or metaphorical—left behind. For example, a purchaser may become accountable for the seller's failure to obtain approval for an alteration to the premises, such as an extension to add a bedroom or patio. I have seen cases where a buyer had to pay thousands of dollars to legalize such an extension, and other cases where the extension had to be torn down and removed. So, make sure that the seller presents you and your attorney with the approvals for all alterations before you close on the property. As far as finding mechanic's liens and other judgments, a lien search should discover whether any of these exist, and the seller will be notified to pay or remove these liens before closing.

INSPECTING FOR AND UNDERSTANDING THE UNDERGROUND OIL TANK

Failing to discover an underground oil tank until after purchase is a common and potentially costly home purchase mistake. If you already know that there is a buried oil tank on the property, you must ask the seller for permission to inspect it and conduct invasive testing.

If the tank has been abandoned (i.e., removed or no longer in use because a new one was installed or the house has been converted to gas heat), you should ask sellers to provide proof that they obtained all permits, inspections, and governmental approvals for either removing the tank or abandoning it in place. Even if the seller makes no mention of such a tank, you must have your inspector test for its presence. An inspector should confirm *in writing* that the home inspection will include a search for an oil tank, and should produce a report stating whether one exists under the property.

If an oil tank is discovered, the buyer needs to understand its significance by learning its age, chances of future leakage, and whether the state's law requires removal as well as maintenance in checking for leaks and using the tank. Many homeowners' insurance policies exclude such tanks from coverage. Unless the seller's policy specifically includes pollution coverage, it's improbable that insurance covers the oil tank, making its removal and maintenance extremely costly. However, proper inspection and accurate representations in the contract of sale avoid this potentially expensive problem. Real estate attorney Leonard Ritz warns: "You cannot rely solely on the information you receive from the seller. Often, the party you purchase the house from is not the original owner, and may not know when the house was converted from oil to gas heat, or whether the tank was properly abandoned."

BUYING A HOME WITH OCCUPANTS OR TENANTS IN POSSESSION

One of the dangers of closing and paying for a home with occupants or tenants still in possession comes from the potential damage that these individuals can do to the home before vacating. Some extreme cases include tenants removing fixtures and large appliances and literally trashing the home. However, most occupants are motivated to leave the property in good condition in order to collect their security deposit upon vacating.

Another danger is that foreclosure situations breed the most outlandish treatment of homes. Of course, the only certain means to prevent this problem would be to purchase the home free of occupants.

On the other hand, if you are buying, for example, a two-family home with the specific hope that the tenants' rent will cover the mortgage payments, then it's beneficial to have a reliable tenant in there. Besides the fact that most occupants are decent human beings who don't want to violate the law, they're also motivated to leave the property in good condition in order to collect their security deposit.

Another strategy to consider when buying a home with occupants is to retain a certain amount of the purchase price in escrow or in an attorney's bank account, pending clearance that no damage has occurred upon exit. You can also take videos and pictures of the home before closing and make sure that your homeowner's insurance policy includes coverage for possible future situations.

PURCHASING A LAND LEASE IN A COOPERATIVE APARTMENT: DETERMINE WHETHER YOU ARE BUYING OR RENTING THE LAND

Although it's relatively uncommon, land leases do exist in some big cities, including New York City. You should check whether your potential unit is affected by a land lease before you purchase. If this is the case, it means that instead of owning the land on which it sits, the cooperative leases this land. Some property owners grant a very long lease—usually at least 100 years—to a developer to build an apartment complex on a large vacant lot. The developer then builds an apartment complex and sells the individual units to the public. The buyers each own their piece of the building for the length of time remaining on the lease. However, if a new lease cannot be negotiated, the landowner can reclaim the land. This will cause the cooperative unit owners to lose their investments in the property and become ordinary rental tenants—or get kicked out altogether.

As a result of this ownership scenario, these land lease apartments usually sell for less than similar conventional properties on the market. If purchasing this kind of unit is a good bet depends on several factors: the length of time remaining on the lease, how much of that time the purchaser plans to be there, and the amount of rent the building pays the developer each year.

As long as you understand the rules, you can consider a cooperative apartment on a land lease a relatively solid investment if 30 years or more are left on the lease and you are planning on being there considerably less than that time. When purchasing a land lease unit, buyers require the assurance that the unit will receive its maximum potential value when selling in the future. A term less than 30 years would likely scare a potential buyer away with thoughts of eviction while in possession. It's important to realize your potential buyer will undergo the fears you experience now tenfold when you are ready to sell the co-op and move on.

Besides the term of the land lease, a potential buyer should also determine the amount of rent the building pays each year. The buyer should study the lease to determine whether any future increases in rent will be within his or her means. When reviewing the building's lease, a buyer should check whether the rent has been predetermined so that owners can reasonably predict their future maintenance payments.

PROPERTY TAXES CAN CHANGE

Be aware of the amount of yearly property taxes, as these can change. Many parts of the country use the transfer of property as an opportunity to reevaluate a home's worth; the taxes on the property may increase or decrease based on this evaluation.

Real estate taxes remain more stable in some states than in others. For instance, in California, property taxes are set at the market value at the time of transfer of ownership. They remain relatively constant throughout the life of that buyer's ownership as a result of a state law titled Proposition 13.

DIFFERENT WAYS TO TAKE TITLE TO THE HOME

How you sign the ownership documents determines not only your ownership interest but also how a property will pass to your heirs upon death. Of course, if you are buying a property by yourself, you can disregard this section. However, it is important for those that put more than one name on the deed or deed of trust (or the stock certificate and proprietary lease for a co-op), to understand the nomenclature surrounding ownership in order to ensure that your wishes are carried out upon a split or death.

Tenants by the Entirety

Tenants by the Entirety is generally only for married couples. This form of ownership states that if one spouse dies, the other automatically inherits full ownership of the property. Upon the sale of the home, proceeds would be allocated equally between the parties.

Tenants by the Entirety provides the additional benefit of offering protection against creditors. The degree of protection varies between states, but generally speaking, if only one spouse owes money to creditors, the creditors will not be able to make any claim on the property. Tenants by the Entirety is not available in all states; these include Colorado, Texas, Maine, Connecticut, North Dakota, South Dakota, Washington, Utah, Wisconsin, Nevada, and South Carolina.

Joint Tenants with Rights of Survivorship

Although the Joint Tenants with Rights of Survivorship (JTWROS) is a popular method of taking title for married couples and partners, it is not necessary to be a married couple or to be in a relationship to take title in this form. JTWROS simply works by granting each party equal ownership in the property. So, in the event of one person's death, the other automatically obtains full ownership of the property. Meaning, if my sister and I bought a home and decided that if one of us dies we would want the other to have full ownership of the property, we would take title in this way.

This method can also be used when more than two parties are taking ownership, for instance, three or more siblings. In the case of three joint tenants, each would own a one-third share. When the first dies, his or her share would be automatically split between the two survivors, leaving them with equal 50 percent ownership. Upon the sale of the home, proceeds would be allocated equally between the parties.

Tenants in Common

Tenants in Common (TIC) gives two or more purchasers an allocated percentage of the property. For example, the distribution could be a 50/50 split between two purchasers, a 70/20/10 split among three purchasers, or however purchasers choose to divide it up. Two or more people can have ownership of the property through this method of taking title. Whereas in both JTWROS and Tenants by the Entirety your portion of the property would automatically pass to the other parties upon your death, TIC dictates that the deceased party's portion of the home be given to the beneficiaries designated in that person's will. For example, my sister, my brother, my father, and I could purchase a home this way and take 25 percent ownership each. If I were to die, my 25 percent would pass to whomever I designate in my will, and each party that has present ownership of the property would still own just their 25 percent.

Upon the sale of a home, proceeds would be split according to each party's designated interest in the property. To that end, TIC may be a better option if one party is going to contribute significantly more money than the other(s) in the purchase of a property in order for that individual to protect his or her interest.

Community Property

In certain states, Community Property is a method of taking ownership designated for married couples only. Each party has an equal share of ownership in the property, and unless any provision in a will indicates otherwise, one party's death leads to the other party inheriting the entire property. Some states require that the surviving spouse undergo a probate court procedure for the property to be transferred to the surviving party. However, most states do not recognize Community Property at all. In fact, the only ones that currently do are Arizona, California, Idaho, Louisiana, Nevada, New Mexico, Texas, Washington, Wisconsin, and the territory of Puerto Rico. Upon the sale of a home, proceeds would be split equally between spouses.

QUICK INSIDER TIP

When couples split, they usually prefer to no longer give financial benefits to their exes. A will can be amended at one party's choosing and a written agreement can have a break-up provision, but deeds are very hard to amend without litigation. So keep this in mind when deciding how to designate each party on the deed, especially if one party is contributing significantly more toward the property.

> ### Advice From My Father
>
> Adam, in Chapter 9 *Hidden Land Mines to Look Out for*, you might mention to visit on a rainy day to check for leaks in ceilings, the roof, and the basement. In the house you were born in I never knew I would have a flood in the basement every time it rained.
>
> I also check now when I am looking for a new house in the shower, many need a new tile job.
>
> I am very proud of you once again, and keep up the good work, love Dad.

FIGURE 9.1   Advice From My Father

Chapter 10 Creative Ways to Get the Seller to Accept Your Below-Market Offer

OFFER ALL CASH OR DO NOT MAKE THE DEAL CONTINGENT ON OBTAINING A LOAN

The victorious home hunter is usually the bidder who offers the highest purchase price. Assuming that two bids are equal, or even if one is slightly lower than the other, the seller is usually motivated to choose the more reliable bidder—the person who demonstrates that he or she has the ability to pay the purchase price. I would personally rather accept a lower bid from a buyer who I'm more confident will close on the home than a higher bid from someone who may not qualify for a mortgage, since this could potentially keep the property tied up for months. An overly generous offer has no value if the buyer cannot come up with the money to purchase the home. The last thing the seller wants in a falling market is to have to put the property back on the market after the deal falls through, especially if prices have dropped since the first offer.

KNOW HOW TO PLAY THE NEGOTIATION GAME: MAKING AND RESPONDING TO THE COUNTER OFFER

One of my chief negotiation strategies is to never make the first offer, as you may be offering more money for the home than the seller planned to accept. Of course, this rarely works in real estate, because you have to counter the sales price that the seller has listed. I am not a fan of offering a number to split in half, or to meet in the middle at a later date; this demonstrates a lack of commitment to a specific amount. Of course, this tactic can be useful at the end of the negotiation when trying to squeeze the last few pennies out of a deal.

I like to provide the lowest counter offer possible without being insulting, so I explain how I got to my number by pulling out comparable home prices and any other useful data I may have collected. I then walk away from the deal for at least 48 to 72 hours. Your response to all calls and e-mails during this time should be that your number is firm and will not be negotiated.

You should also mention that although you will continue home-shopping, you would prefer the negotiated property upon the acceptance of your offer. You should not call the homeowner during this time as you will appear weak, and your actions will reveal that your number could go higher.

Despite the fact that this method of negotiation can yield amazing results, it's not for everyone. I have lost more than one property this way. If you can't handle the possibility of losing the property, you should simply ask the broker how low a price the seller will accept. If you can afford it, and if your heart is truly set on the property, then offer to pay this amount. You will be surprised at how often you can obtain a straight answer from the broker. For example, one broker knew that he was losing the exclusive rights to sell a property, so he told my client exactly how low an offer the seller would accept so that he could close the deal and obtain the commission. There is usually an advantage in talking to the broker, since they occasionally provide hints and other information that may help you prepare a counter offer.

GET THE FIRST CALL WHEN THE PRICE DROPS: GIVE SELLERS YOUR PRICE AND ASK THEM TO CALL YOU WHEN THE ASKING PRICE FALLS

Among the many properties you will view on your way to becoming a housing market expert will probably be one that will never sell any-where *near* its asking price. The key to negotiating when you fall in love with an overpriced home like this is to persuade the seller to call you first when the property's price drops within your range. Try to discuss the situation with the seller. Obtain the seller's contact infor-mation and follow up with an e-mail, or you can hand the seller a card with your phone number along with the price you would pay.

In order to encourage the call, the figure you choose should be the exact highest number you are ready to spend on the home. The key is to get the first call before the next open house or listing of the price reduction. Your goal is to get the home into contract and taken off the market before any showings occur. However, if you receive this coveted phone call and try to further negotiate down the sales price, you will most likely kill the deal, since the seller will become frus-trated with a further rejection after making great efforts to sell the home. I know one person who took this approach and who kept negotiating despite my advice to the contrary. The following week-end, 47 different parties visited the home. With so many bidders, the broker scheduled best and final offers to be in by Wednesday—and my friend never received another call.

BECOME THE REAL ESTATE BROKER'S BEST FRIEND

Another tactic to help you eventually claim a coveted home is to become the broker's best friend. After you've visited the home, tried to negotiate the price and failed on the first visit, check in with the broker periodically. Let him know that you have an interest in the prop-erty, but only if it falls within a certain price range. If the broker is e-mail friendly, send an e-mail from time to time and follow up with a phone call when you want to secure more information on the status of the sale.

Your goal is to be the first person the agent remembers—and therefore, calls—when the sale price drops. Many times, the seller will reconsider a previously rejected offer shortly after the showing, especially when there have been no other offers or low open house attendance.

BRING YOUR FINANCIAL RESUME TO DEMONSTRATE YOUR ABILITY TO CLOSE ON THE HOME

Have your financial resume handy when negotiating a purchase in person in order to demonstrate your economic ability to buy a home. Organize any related financial material so that you can supply it upon demand to prove how fiscally attractive you are. A good rule of thumb is to bring the same documents your bank requests during the application process and at least one pre-approval letter. Since this information is private, do not leave it with the seller or broker. Instead, keep it collated in a notebook or document so that you can present it quickly and easily. Make sure that your financial information has been thoroughly purged of any account and identification numbers or any other information that could assist thieves in stealing your identity.

THE RIGHT OF FIRST REFUSAL

If you are renting a home that you may one day wish to buy, you might want to ask the landlord-seller for the right to match any other offer on the home. The seller will want to enter into such an agreement only when it is financially beneficial; the most opportune time for such an agreement would be when signing the lease. Such an agreement would give you, as the tenant-buyer, a short amount of time to match any third party's offer for the property. Many times, the landlord-seller will remember the right of first refusal or the tenant's interest in purchasing the premises, and will simply offer the tenant the property without even waiting for other offers. Remember to make sure that you have agreed upon the right of first refusal *in writing* in order to enforce the provision.

BUYER FLEXIBILITY: LEARN THE SELLER'S MOVING PREFERENCES

Sellers sometimes have interests other than obtaining the highest purchase price that may be priorities in the sale. Some of these include the date of the sale of the property, the moving date, or even a requirement for temporary storage space. When two similar offers have been made for a home, the bidder who demonstrates flexibility in the finer details of the transaction could end up winning. For example, many sellers need cash quickly for many reasons, such as to ward off foreclosure, pay for a college education, or allow a child to finish a school year. These sellers may be looking for buyers that will allow them to live in the home for a number of months after title has been transferred to the buyer. Other times, the seller may not want to have the sale occur for a number of months. Being accommodating to the seller's wishes may put you at a distinct advantage over other potential buyers. Additional small gestures—granting the seller temporary storage space or providing a service like setting up computer or television equipment—may endear the seller to your offer above all others.

ENDEAR THE SELLER THROUGH THOUGHTFUL GESTURES AND REMEMBERING NAMES AND LIFE EVENTS

When owners sell homes personally or attend a home showing, try to learn as much as you can about them and their interests without being intrusive. The smallest gestures—like bringing a mentioned favorite cake or a certain kind of coffee, flowers, or wine on the second visit—could make the seller consciously or subconsciously root for you to capture the home. Bringing tickets to the seller's favorite sports team can do wonders for a negotiation.

Remembering sellers and their kids' names, ages, and hobbies also can help to make you the favorite. In truth, it's extremely rare for the highest price *not* to win the home when no other significant considerations are involved. However, some thoughtful deeds may prompt the seller to call you first if the deal falls through and the price drops significantly at a later date.

In addition, fewer disputes usually arise over details of the sale—such as which items are being included—when the seller and buyer get along well. Sellers who like you are also more likely to provide you with tips on how to operate the home, where to shop and dine in the neighborhood, and how to get around most pleasantly and efficiently.

PLACE AN AD OR CREATE A WEB SITE OR COMMERCIAL

This is especially important for those buying many properties and interested in creating wealth in real estate: An advertisement, Web site, or television commercial may help you to secure a property even before it officially hits the market. This works especially well in down markets with frequent foreclosures; the person advertising may get a call from someone who does not have the time or resources to list the property on the market. Although we neither endorse nor condemn it, one memorable example is a company with a Web site titled Webuy uglyhouses.com. This company has a commercial combined with a Web site soliciting offers on properties. These tactics are usually most useful for buying in markets with high foreclosure rates; however, I applaud that level of creativity when and wherever it shows up.

CHAPTER SUMMARY AND INSIDER TIPS

- The seller is usually motivated to choose the more reliable bidder. I would personally rather accept a lower bid from a buyer who I am more confident will close on the home than a higher bid from someone who may not qualify for a mortgage. An overly generous offer has no value if the buyer cannot come up with the money to purchase the home.

- I am not a fan of offering a number to split in half, or to meet in the middle at a later date; this demonstrates a lack of commitment to a specific amount. I like to provide the lowest counter offer possible without being insulting, so I explain how I got to my number by pulling out comparable home prices and any other useful data I may have collected. I then walk away from the deal for at least 48 to 72 hours. Your response to all calls and e-mails during this time should be that your number is firm and will not be negotiated.

- If you can't handle the possibility of losing the property, you should simply ask the broker how low a price the seller will accept. If you can afford it, and if your heart is truly set on the property, then offer to pay this amount. You will be surprised at how often you can obtain a straight answer from the broker.
- The key to negotiating when you fall in love with an overpriced home is to persuade the seller to call you first when the property's price drops. Hand the seller a card with your phone number along with the exact highest price you would pay.
- Be accessible. The seller you were hoping to buy from could come to terms with some other prospective buyer during the time it takes for you to return a phone call. I return all calls within 24 hours, and usually within minutes. When trying to scoop a deal, try to be accessible immediately.
- Have your financial resume handy when negotiating a purchase in person in order to demonstrate your economic ability to buy a home.
- If you are renting a home that you may one day wish to buy, you might want to ask the landlord-seller for the right to match any other offer on the home. Many times, the landlord-seller will remember this right of first refusal or the tenant's interest in purchasing the premises, and will simply offer the tenant the property without even waiting for other offers.
- When two similar offers have been made for a home, the bidder who demonstrates flexibility in the finer details of the transaction could end up winning.
- The smallest gestures—like bringing a mentioned favorite cake or a certain kind of coffee, flowers, or wine on the second visit—could make the seller consciously or subconsciously root for you to capture the home.

Chapter 11 Negotiating a Great Deal on a Newly Constructed Property

What You Must Know Before Signing the Contract to Purchase

Homes that are many years old should be thoroughly battle-tested. Chances are that the current owners know all about the home's creaks and leaks. Many newly constructed homes have not been so tested; they haven't undergone a stormy winter or a hot summer to uncover potential leaks and see whether structural systems are working properly. To that end, purchasing newly constructed property requires special care to prevent problems upon moving into the new home.

This does not mean that new homes are in any way inferior to older, age-tested properties. In fact, someone purchasing newly constructed property is frequently obtaining a home with the most technologically advanced electrical, ventilation, and air conditioning systems. New homes often include the latest appliances, fixtures, plumbing, and big ticket items such as a new boiler or roof. In older homes, the eventual replacement/repair cost for these items can be significant. Buyers also occasionally have the option to customize a new construction to their exact specifications. It's important, however, to remove any rose-colored glasses and follow the suggestions in this chapter to protect yourself when purchasing a newly constructed property.

CONDUCT AN EXTENSIVE INSPECTION OF THE PREMISES USING A QUALIFIED INSPECTOR/ENGINEER

Many new home nightmares can be prevented by using the services of a reputable and qualified inspector/engineer or architect prior to closing on the property. These professionals draft reports that may cover many common home problems, such as the potential for repetitive flooding, buckling wood floors, inoperable windows, non-functional heating, damaged fixtures, leaky roofs, fire code violations, inadequate air conditioning, and a host of other issues. The most common setbacks also tend to be the most expensive to repair. These big-ticket items include the roof, boiler, and elevators (in large buildings).

A qualified inspector should be able to furnish a written report of any structural and even minor problems involving the property. If the inspector/engineer has not completed the report before contract negotiation, the contract should include a provision allowing the buyer to cancel the contract at least two weeks after signing if the home has serious structural problems. Although many builders will not allow any negotiation of the contract of sale, you should also try to include a provision that states you are not required to close or purchase the property until all problems listed in the report and on the pre-closing inspection *punch list* have been fixed. This should help ensure that the property into which you're moving is free of defects, potentially saving you thousands of dollars.

I recommend a three-phase inspection for newly constructed properties. The first should occur after completion of the framing of the property. The second inspection should occur after all cooling and heating systems, plumbing, and electrical equipment are in place, but before the sheetrock is installed. The final inspection should occur immediately before the closing.

Although not a total panacea, hiring an inspector/engineer is a wise investment. The cost for this service is minimal compared to the expenses related to taking the builder to court or repairing the problems on your own dime.

KNOW THE BUILDER'S PAST PERFORMANCES

When buying a newly constructed property, building, or an apartment therein, your only available image of the property at contract signing may be a dot on a map of the building plans, and a view of the vacant land where the property will soon be built. It's therefore impossible in that moment to ensure that your home will be built properly—with correctly installed fixtures, appliances in good working order, and all other safe and usable features. That is why inquiring into the builder's record is essential. Obtain and call references from the builder, and request a list of other properties that they have previously developed. Take the time to visit one of these properties and inquire about the residents' satisfaction level. These few small tasks will assist in ensuring that your future home will be built with the care and quality described in the builder's brochure.

OBTAIN WARRANTIES FROM THE BUILDER

Most home sales dictate that the seller is longer obliged to fix problems once the keys and ownership documents have been transferred. However, a number of states require builders to remedy post-closing repair issues for newly constructed or rehabilitated properties. Though some of these states decree that repair protections and warranty enforcement be granted to buyers of newly constructed properties, others are not so generous when certain warranties are waived in the contract of sale. Depending on the building's size and the state in which it is located, warranties of the property's plumbing, electrical, heating, cooling, and ventilation systems are enforced for at least one or two years. Additionally, some states issue other basic warranties requiring that the property be built in a skillful manner and that it remain safe and habitable for additional years.

You should attempt to obtain warranties from the builder for all appropriate items; without a contract provision stating that you are to receive these, you could end up paying for repairs yourself. Thus, preventing financial devastation lies in your ability to have the contract of sale include as many warranty protections as you can negotiate.

THE BRAND NAMES AND THE APPLIANCES AND FIXTURES INSTALLED SHOULD BE ITEMIZED IN THE CONTRACT OF SALE

In order to get the greatest value from your new construction, the contract of sale should specify which fixtures and appliances are to be installed in the property. Since it is important that these amenities are well made and durable, ensure that the contract includes the brand names of the appliances and fixtures.

THE MOST COMMON PROBLEM WHEN PURCHASING A NEW CONSTRUCTION: THE MOVE-IN DATE

The chances of moving into your new home on the date that the builder predicted are probably close to the odds of winning the lottery. This common problem can be very disruptive to your schedule and interfere with plans to vacate your current residence, or when your children might start at a new school, plus many other considerations. The numerous reasons for delays may include erratic weather, shortages of materials, and other unpredicted problems that can occur during construction, making it almost impossible for the builder to specify an exact completion time.

The good news is that you may be able to add provisions to your contract to make your life easier if such a delay occurs. One such provision should state that if the property is not in move-in condition by a certain date, you may either cancel the contract and receive the return of all monies or obtain a reduction in the purchase price.

Many new construction contracts require the buyer to close upon obtaining a temporary certificate of occupancy. However, in many jurisdictions, a builder can acquire this certificate while the building is under construction and not even close to completion. You may therefore want to revise this contract clause accordingly, and attempt to negotiate a closing date only *after* the home is completely constructed and in move-in condition. Also you should negotiate a date by which time the buyer can cancel the contract of sale if the home is still not finished.

LOCKING IN AN INTEREST RATE

Another concern in the delay of a closing date is losing a favorable interest rate that you have locked in with your bank. Most banks charge additional fees to extend the interest rate after a certain period of time, while others do not permit any such extension. If you do not extend your interest rate, the new one may be higher, thus costing you thousands of dollars over the life of the loan. Have the builder agree to pay all added costs associated with your loan if the property is not ready to close on time. If the builder cannot close on time, attempt to have the builder himself agree to help you obtain an extension of your commitment locked at the previous rate before it expired. Most importantly, do not close until the premises have been inspected and you are satisfied that the construction is free from defects. If you are obtaining a bank loan, make sure your contract requires the builder to satisfy the bank's conditions and requirements before you are obligated to close.

By following the above recommendations, buying a newly constructed property should result in a wonderful home purchase experience.

MY STORY: THE IMPORTANCE OF HIRING AN ENGINEER

"John, how many of these meetings have we been to?" I inquired of my law partner, John Desiderio.

"Well, at least 50, but I really don't know. Too many," John answered.

"Well, any time I get a group of people to listen to me, I'm happy. I remember a few years ago you would grade my performance after these meetings. I usually got a C," I mused.

"You deserved it back then. As far as this meeting, don't ask me questions that I might not be able to answer. And stop calling me the 'Ivy

(continued)

(*continued*)

League lawyer'!" he said. "You're young enough to be my son. So I can grade you whenever I want."

John and I made an interesting team at these meetings. As a street lawyer, I tend to use my passion just as much as my brains for every case. I would quote to John an Italian adage, not only because of his Italian heritage, but because it reflects one of his greatest strengths: "*Chi va piano, va sano e va lontano,*" which means, "Those that go slow, go safely and far." John is the very personification of that thought. He would always carefully read documents and give considerable thought to any topic before forming an opinion on it.

We were in the car on our way to a homeowner's association meeting. We had prepared for the meeting as if it were a job interview to win the chance to represent the homeowners in their struggle to get the newly constructed building in the condition promised to them in the marketing materials. Because of the real estate boom, many builders had cut corners in the actual construction of the building on land they had expensively purchased in order to allow room for a profit. This had led to many very poorly constructed buildings and many ensuing lawsuits.

Half an hour later, I walked into a homeowner's association meeting attended by more than 100 people. One of the leaders introduced us and said a few words as to why they intended to hire our firm to battle the developer. Then it was my turn to speak.

"Hello. Thank you. I am the person who will be taking lots of your money that you should be spending on anything else, and instead be using it to fund my future kids' college educations."

I wasn't just going for the chuckles; I wanted these people to know that I realized how disgusted they were at having to hire me. I proceeded to tell them my game plan for getting their building to the condition that the builder originally promised in the marketing materials.

"How many of you hired an engineer to inspect the building before closing on your new home?" I asked.

Only one hand reached into the sky.

Despite my years of experience in this field, it never ceases to amaze me how many buyers of a newly constructed building—a structure that has never been lived in or tested—will choose their new homes based only on some marketing materials and a dot on a building plan.

It's likely the biggest purchase of their lives, and these poor folks have given their life savings without even getting a detailed inspection of the home and building in return.

I started detailing my game plan for the building by comparing it to our successes in other buildings. I shared with them their rights under the law, as well as their limited weapons to convince the builder to provide the home as promised.

"So I understand that you have a few problems with your building," I continued, and then repeated what I understood these concerns to be. The engineer had reported building issues with the air conditioning, heating system, roof, and hot water—all of which were actually pretty typical. The big ticket items in most buildings usually include the roof, boiler, and elevator, because these are the most expensive items to repair. Among the building's other problems were the lack of insulation between the walls, a roof that did not repel water, and hundreds of safety violations: a cockloft where the builder failed to place fire-prevention material between one unit's ceiling and the floor of the unit above it, giving residents about 30 seconds—instead of the required three minutes—to escape a fire.

I discussed their options, the time frame during which the building might be fixed, the different scenarios that could occur, and the possible costs involved.

"You have a very good team of leaders," I continued. "You have completed the most important step: hiring an engineer to analyze the building's problems. You've launched an Internet group to exchange e-mails with each other, and begun to document the problems. By sharing this information with each other, many of you will learn about problems that you did not realize existed in your unit."

I added some humor to this very serious discussion by sharing the top ten things the developer may do to avoid fixing the building, and by mentioning that the attorney general had sued only three developers. I explained that Attorney-General-turned-Governor Eliot Spitzer's administration was apparently too busy doing other things when he could have been suing crooked developers (as this was right around the time that Spitzer was caught participating in a prostitution ring).

As I continued speaking, I was about to ask one owner why he was wearing sunglasses at night indoors. However, I caught myself before the words came out when I realized that he was blind. Doing a quick about-face, I immediately continued answering questions.

Walking out of the building I asked both John and the manager of the building, Brandon Wechsler, how we did. "Well," Brandon volunteered, "You were about to ask a blind guy why he was wearing sunglasses. Otherwise, you were spot on as they really needed to hear what you had to say."

John offered his two cents. "You have done worse. You had some good moments, and you spoke well—much slower than you used to speak."

(continued)

(*continued*)

"I really just feel for these owners," I answered. "Imagine if these families had a decent engineer inspect the building before purchasing? They would be saving a lot of money on legal fees and even possibly keeping their families from harm's way."

"I give you a B+. Now let's get this building fixed," John concluded as we drove back to our homes.

CHAPTER SUMMARY AND INSIDER TIPS

- Do not close on a newly constructed home without a certificate of occupancy or, at a minimum, making sure that it's a habitable dwelling. Make sure the contract of sale specifies that the buyer cannot be forced to close until the home is habitable and holds either a temporary or final certificate of occupancy.

- For newly constructed properties that are not near completion, the exact move-in date in the contract of sale is a fiction. Until the property is near completion, any builder will tell you it is impossible to predict the move-in date. You should negotiate the ability to cancel your contract if you cannot move in after one year from signing the contract of sale.

- If the property does not close when promised, request that the builder pay for any additional financing costs incurred, including increased interest rate costs.

- Especially for complexes of over 100 units, federal and state laws and regulations may supersede or amend the purchaser's rights applicable to the home. For example, The Interstate Land Sales Full Disclosure Act requires the builder to complete construction of the home within two years, or the buyer is given the ability to cancel the contract of sale and get back the down payment.

- Make sure that you negotiate warranties into the contract of sale. Ideally, these warranties should last for a number of years so that you do not end up paying out of your own pocket to fix faulty items prematurely. Additionally, make sure that you obtain copies of all related warranties and proof of their lifespan.

- Buyers will often negotiate items that do not require extra costs or for monies to be spent. A developer may be willing to provide an outdoor shower, the enlargement of one room versus another, a carpeted basement, or additional electrical sockets—especially if the purchaser is willing to pay any extra costs. Of course, you must make these kinds of requests before the property is built.

- Condominium rules undergo substantial changes very infrequently. This stems from the condominium association's corporate documents, which usually require a majority or 66 percent of unit owners to change the regulations. If you are specifically concerned about a particular issue when buying, you should inquire about it before purchasing the home.

- For major projects, you'll want to find out whether or not the construction is adequately financed. Discover whether the builder has enough working capital and monies set aside to cover the costs of building the home. If possible, review their financial statements and learn about their funding sources, such as lenders.

- For larger buildings especially, inspecting the unit alone is not enough. Make sure that your inspector/engineer also has access to the big ticket items, which include the boiler, the roof, and the elevators, if applicable, when inspecting multi-family dwellings.

PART Three

GETTING UNCOMMON DEALS ON CLOSING COSTS

Chapter 12 The Closing Map
A Guide to Finding and Buying a Home

This chapter is a general guide on what a buyer and seller need to know to understand the home purchase and sale process, as well as to assist in making the very best real estate decisions. It includes descriptions of the various typical events and occurrences that take place during the real estate closing process.

> Please note that even though, in some areas of the country, title agencies or escrow and settlement agents' services are used instead of an attorney, this chapter is written assuming that the buyer is using an attorney for the home purchase.

OBTAINING FINANCING

You should be in touch with a lender from the time you start thinking about looking for a new home. As we emphasized at the beginning of the book, you should never go shopping without knowing how much you have to spend. Using a buyer's financial qualifications, which include yearly income as well as assets and liabilities, a conversation with a lender should provide an estimate of how much a bank will be able to loan a buyer. Of course, only buyers themselves can decide the appropriate monthly payment they can afford to pay a lender without risking distress or foreclosure.

By following the advice in Chapter 1, *Get Ready to Buy: Tools and Suggestions to Maximize Buying and Borrowing Power*, you should have obtained a lender's pre-approval letter. This comes from a prospective lender who is agreeing to lend you the money for your new home, provided that you satisfy a list of conditions before they do so. A pre-approval letter is not a commitment letter, it merely states that the lender would *consider* making a loan if certain conditions are met. Examples of some of these standard conditions are: verification by the lender of your income and employment history; verification that an appraisal of the home values it high enough to justify the amount of the prospective loan; and that there is no change in your financial circumstances—for example, that you have not lost your job or incurred substantial new debt. Many other stipulations may be included. Read your pre-approval letter carefully and, if in doubt, discuss these conditions with your attorney.

Having this kind of pre-approval on hand will show any potential seller that you are serious about buying a home, something that can give you an edge if more than one person is making an offer on the property. Again, it is important to note that the pre-approval letter merely states that the lender is *interested* in making a loan to you. It has no legal significance, and is not a guarantee that you will receive a commitment from the lender. This will only happen once, if and when all conditions have been met.

MAKING THE OFFER

Once you have found and made an offer on a desirable home, this information is generally passed on either to the seller or the real estate broker. The offer to purchase typically includes the property's address, along with the buyer's current address and, in a number of states, the social security number. In addition, it will indicate the amount of both the offer and the down payment, and the estimated date when you believe you will be ready to pay the purchase price for the home, formally known as the *closing date*. As the buyer, you should also indicate whether the purchase is contingent upon obtaining a mortgage. Until this offer to purchase becomes immortalized in writing and signed by the buyer and seller via the contract of sale, both parties may withdraw their offer and acceptance. The ability to revoke an offer and acceptance demonstrates the importance of executing the contract of sale.

In most states, a contract to purchase real property must be in writing. It is important to understand that until a written contract of sale acceptable to both parties has been signed by both parties, there is no enforceable agreement.

HIRING AN ATTORNEY

In order to limit any delays in selling their home, sellers should have an attorney ready to close the deal as soon as they place the property on the market. Buyers must have an attorney lined up as soon as they are ready to make an offer on the property, and they would be wise to have one as soon as they start home shopping. Remember that until a contract is executed by both buyer and seller, the parties can withdraw their offers, and the sellers can either take the property off the market or sell it to someone else. To ensure success in buying a home, it is important to have the real estate professionals ready to go to work. Please refer to the discussion on hiring an attorney in Chapter 14, *Finding, Hiring, and Utilizing an Aggressive Attorney*.

THE ACCEPTANCE OF THE OFFER AND DRAFTING OF THE CONTRACT OF SALE

At the time your offer is accepted, you will usually need to give the seller or real estate broker your attorney's contact information. This will allow him or her to review the basic terms of the sale with the seller's attorney and request that a proposed contract of sale be sent to him. The seller's attorney will then prepare the contract and send it to the buyer's attorney for review and comments.

Depending on where the property is located, much of the information included in the contract of sale may come from a document the broker has prepared, called a *deal sheet*. The deal sheet should include the seller and purchasers' names, respective attorneys, the brokers, the purchase price, and the amount of the down payment. The deal sheet should also be very specific about the particulars of the transaction, some of which include: the closing date, whether the transaction is contingent upon the purchaser obtaining financing, and any fixtures or seller's personal property included in the transaction. For example, wall mounted televisions, stereo equipment, window treatments, built-ins, and chandeliers may or may not be incorporated into the sale. Future possessory rights to any items desired that are already in the home should be specifically listed in the contract of sale.

The custom in certain localities is for the buyer's broker to use a form prepared by the local Board of Realtors or Bar Association. This document has the same details as the deal sheet, but in the form of an enforceable contract. However, these contracts are usually subject to attorney approval on both sides. Depending on the deal, the attorney may then draw a contract from scratch, modify the broker's form, or leave the form as is.

SIGNING THE CONTRACT OF SALE AND MAKING THE CONTRACT DEPOSIT

Upon signing the contract of sale, the purchaser delivers the originals to his or her attorney, who will forward these together with the contract deposit to the seller's attorney. As discussed earlier, the contract deposit is customarily 10 percent of the purchase price. The buyer and seller usually sign four original copies of the contract. The contract deposit may be in the form of a personal check; it is usually made out to either the seller's attorney—as *escrow agent* or *as attorney*—the real estate broker, or the title company. The buyer's attorney should submit the contract deposit to the seller's attorney with written instructions that the contract deposit is not to be deposited until the seller has countersigned the contract, and two fully executed copies have been delivered to the purchaser or his attorney. One of these copies is for your attorney's file, and the other is for you. The buyer's deposit may then be deposited into the seller's attorney's escrow account (a special bank account for holding money belonging to someone other than the attorney). The deposit protects the seller in the event that the buyer walks away from or is unable to complete the transaction. At the closing, the contract deposit will be credited against the purchase price.

INSURANCE AND TAX ESCROW

If you obtain a loan to purchase the home, it's likely that the lender will require you to maintain a tax and insurance escrow account (also called *impounds* in some states). At closing, the lender will take *a cushion* of a few months of taxes and insurance payments from you to be retained as an excess amount in your lender's account under your name. For a full discussion of the insurance and tax escrow account, please see Chapter 2, *How to Get the Cheapest Loan at the Best Rate*.

THE MORTGAGE CONTINGENCY CLAUSE AND OTHER CONTINGENCIES

Among the terms in the contract of sale, the mortgage contingency clause deserves particular attention. This section allows buyers to cancel the contract if they are unable to obtain a mortgage within a fixed period of time. When faced with two equal buyers, a seller will usually choose the one that agrees to waive this clause. However, buyers should only agree to remove this section if they have the liquid funds on hand, readily accessible, to pay the purchase price on the closing date. The timing of the events during the contingency period is vital as failure to meet deadlines may force you to forfeit your contract deposit and suffer other monetary damages.

Customarily, buyers will have between 30 and 45 days to obtain a loan commitment letter from the date that their attorneys receive a fully executed contract of sale. The loan commitment letter proves that the lender has committed to giving you the financing required as long as you fulfill certain conditions. If a buyer is unable to obtain an appropriate mortgage and commitment letter within the contracted amount of time, the buyer's attorney has the options of sending a notice to the seller's attorney to cancel the contract (whereby the contract deposit must be returned to the buyer); requesting additional time for the buyer to attempt to qualify for the necessary loan; or waiving the mortgage contingency.

If any complications occur in obtaining a loan, buyers must immediately communicate this information to their attorneys to save the buyer's down payment. For example, if the buyer's attorney attempts to cancel the time limits in the contract of sale to obtain the commitments without canceling or extending the period, the seller will not have a legal duty to return the down payment. In addition to keeping the down payment, the seller could also potentially sell the property to someone else, or—depending on the contract of sale—even sue the buyer to close title to purchase the home.

Other contingencies in the contract of sale vary depending on the state of the purchase. For instance, in some states, including California, a standard contract of sale may allow the opportunity for the buyer to cancel the contract if the property appraises at less than the purchase price. Wherever possible, I highly recommend adding a clause that allows you to cancel the transaction if the property appraises below your contract's purchase price.

THE CLOSING DATE

Whether your children need to be in their new home by the start of school or you need to move out of your present home because your lease is ending, you will want to confirm your closing date. This is the date on which a buyer obtains the keys to the new home, and it is customarily listed in the contract of sale.

Many homebuyers are shocked and disgruntled to learn that the date listed for the closing in the contract of sale can still be delayed by either party for many weeks or even a month. Actually, the closing date in the contract is usually an *on or about* closing date. This loosely termed date usually benefits a buyer that may not be able to obtain financing for the home or sell a former home by a certain date. Despite this closing flexibility, a buyer's or seller's attorney has the ability, after a reasonable delay of the closing, to send a *time of the essence* letter setting a firm date, time, and place when the closing must occur, or the other party is in default.

Buyers and sellers who must close by a certain date will want this date included in the contract of sale with the legal warning words deeming the date time of the essence, which makes postponing the closing date a risky endeavor. No matter the reason or the excuse then, if the closing does not occur by the contracted date, the purchaser or seller will be deemed in default of the contract of sale. The down payment may be forfeited or the contract cancelled and the seller obligated to refund the down payment.

THE ENGINEER

Once an accepted offer or executed contract of sale is received, a licensed engineer or home inspector should be hired to determine the physical condition of the home. A full discussion on the benefits of this, as well as tips on how to maximize an engineer's utility, can be found in Chapter 13, *Using the Home Inspection to Lower the Price.*

DUE DILIGENCE FOR COOPERATIVE AND CONDOMINIUM PURCHASES

If you are purchasing a condominium or a cooperative apartment and your verbal offer has been accepted, your attorney should begin the process of what is commonly referred to as *due diligence*. This will include a review of the cooperative or condominium's organizational documents, the offering plan and amendments, and the minutes of the annual shareholder's or unit owner's board meetings. For a full discussion of due diligence see Chapter 14, *Finding, Hiring, and Utilizing an Aggressive Attorney.*

REVIEWING THE BUILDING'S FINANCIALS

Your attorney must also review the cooperative's financial statements for the past two years. An ideal building will have sound financials, and the statements will let you know whether the building has heavy reserves or monetary savings, has no reserves at all, or has a history of special assessments and minimal reserves (in which case, the building may not have enough if a problem occurs). Ideally, the minimum amount of reserves should be enough to cover two months' maintenance payments. Careful review of the footnotes will disclose outstanding obligations, such as a mortgage (or mortgages) for a co-op or a condominium association loan and any outstanding litigation.

TERMITE INSPECTION

If you are purchasing a private residence, you will be allowed to conduct a termite inspection once both you and the seller have signed the contract. The termite inspection company should perform a thorough inspection of the home and attempt to assess termite and other wood boring insect damage, if any. Many home inspection companies will conduct this inspection as well. In the event that there is considerable damage or evidence of infestation, the company will indicate the severity and prepare a suggestion to eliminate it. Usually, the contract of sale stipulates that the seller is obligated to repair the damage if it is below a certain maximum amount of money. In the event that the damage is in excess of that amount, the seller will have the option to cancel the contract. Should the seller opt to do so, however, purchasers may still agree to proceed with the transaction if they choose to have the damage repaired at their own cost, or manage to negotiate a proper credit at closing. If you contemplate using such an option, be sure that you estimate a realistic cost.

Of course several different contract provisions can be written with regard to whether and when the purchaser or seller can cancel the contract. Many of these negotiated provisions are as creative as the different types of people and properties involved in the transactions. Remember at the contract stage to always remain on guard and mindful of protecting your interests in the transaction; hope for the best and expect the worst. For more discussion on this topic, see the section entitled "Protecting Yourself When Signing the Contract of Sale" in Chapter 13, *Using the Home Inspection to Lower the Price.*

BOARD APPLICATIONS

Cooperative Apartment Purchase: Board Approval

When purchasing a cooperative apartment, you are usually required to submit an application to the building's board. The contract of sale usually provides that your completed application be submitted to the board within 10 to 15 business days following the receipt of the fully executed contract. This period may be modified depending on whether or not the board requires that a copy of your loan commitment letter be included with your application.

These applications can be highly invasive; they require that you share personal financial information, including copies of financial statements and tax returns as well as personal and financial references. They also require you to provide additional personal information about the people that will be residing in the apartment. If you're using an agent, have him or her assist you with the package; many of them are experts in this area and have helped numerous buyers in the past in completing these packages successfully. In many states and counties, condominium board applications are customarily not as invasive as cooperative applications, if they are required at all.

Condominiums with a right of first refusal in their organization may require a similar application to cooperatives, and the trend seems to indicate that some condo applications are just as intrusive as those required by co-ops. In most cases, the condominium boards are not likely to exercise the right of first refusal, and in most instances such exercise would require a vote of the unit owners.

TITLE INSURANCE AND LIEN SEARCH

Once you have a legally binding contract, your attorney will order a title report in the case of a private residence or a condominium, or a lien search in the case of a cooperative apartment.

In my humble opinion, title insurance is better than car or accident insurance. Unlike traditional insurance, title insurance starts protecting a buyer before the closing of the purchase. First, title insurers work to ensure sure that you will be the rightful owner of the property and second, title insurers participate like a tax or money collector in removing all liens, judgments, and any other encumbrances so that you will not owe someone else's debts at the time you receive the keys to your new home. So instead of paying for a loss after it happens, title insurers do their homework so a loss never occurs. And only if a mistake is made or a fraud or other illegal activity is missed by the insurer will the title company pay to defend you in court and if a loss occurs, the title insurer will pay.

For a full discussion on the role and benefits of title insurance and lien abstracts, please turn to Chapter 17, *The Purchase of Title Insurance*.

THE BOARD INTERVIEW

When purchasing a cooperative apartment, the loan commitment letter should be the last remaining item needed to complete your application. After the board receives this letter, they will get together and review your application. Once they have reviewed it, you will be required to attend a personal board interview. During this interview you may be asked questions, including issues raised by your application, such as your financial ability to afford the unit. Understand that since the interview may be the key to rejecting your purchase, the interview should definitely not be treated as a confession. Do your homework; learn about the building through means outside of the interview. The board of directors' minutes of meetings, financial reports, and interviews with residents and real estate professionals should provide you with a great deal of information on the building. Questions you pose during the interview—if any—should be kept to a minimum. You want to dress professionally or in a conservative manner, and follow all normal courtesy protocols. Very few applicants are rejected for not speaking enough at the interview.

OBTAINING THE RIGHT OF POSSESSION OF THE HOME

Once all remaining loan conditions have been satisfied, and the cooperative has approved your application—or the condominium board has waived its right of first refusal in the case of a condominium purchase—it is time to attend the real estate closing to complete your purchase of the home.

Your attorney will schedule the closing with the seller and lender's attorneys and the building's managing agent. A closing for a co-op apartment will take place at the managing agent's office, whereas one for a condominium or single family home may take place at the seller's or lender's attorney's office, or at a mutually convenient location.

THE CLOSING

Preparation for Closing

For a private residence or a condominium transaction, your attorney will also coordinate the closing with the title insurance company. This will ensure that a representative will attend the closing in order to review the documents, collect them for recording, and to issue the title insurance policy or policies.

The actual closing date may differ substantially from that cited in the contract of sale. Make sure that both parties are aware of delays, as scheduling a closing involves many variables. The actual date and time is contingent on a number of components, including the closing date in the contract, the availability of the purchaser, seller, lender, manager, and their attorneys, as well as how quickly the sellers can arrange to have their belongings removed from the property. Additionally, it may take a considerable period of time for a cooperative apartment board to schedule your interview and report the results. It's entirely possible for these reasons—and countless potential others—that the date of the actual closing will be later than that established in the contract.

This is also the time to resolve all questions about how and when anyone—particularly the seller—will be making repairs to the home. It is customary for the purchaser to conduct an inspection of the property immediately (usually within 24 hours) prior to the closing to confirm that they are receiving the property in the condition required under the contract.

About a day prior to the closing, your lender's attorney should forward your attorney a list of the lender's fees and charges. This will indicate exactly how much money you may access from your loan. Your attorney will then send you a detailed list of the closing costs, along with what checks (certified or bank checks) you need to bring to pay the balance of the purchase price still due to the seller, if any, after your mortgage proceeds have been allocated. In addition, the statement from your attorney should have a breakdown of your anticipated title insurance charges, as well as any charges imposed by the managing agent if you are purchasing a cooperative apartment.

When real estate professionals say *certified funds* they are speaking of certified checks, bank checks, teller's checks, money orders, cash, or other means of payment that are presumably safer than a personal check. For some transactions in some locations, an attorney's trust fund check may suffice for this purpose.

The Real Estate Closing

For states in which the seller and buyer get together to transfer title, a good real estate closing can be compared to a party—and everyone should bring something to the event. All of the parties meet, execute transfer documents, and the purchaser pays the balance of what is owed to the seller.

If the closing is for a private residence or a condominium, the seller will sign a deed and any applicable documents that transfer ownership of the property to the purchaser. For cooperative apartments, sellers will surrender their original stock certificate and proprietary lease. Purchasers will execute their own new proprietary lease (some cooperative corporations accomplish this by just assigning the old proprietary lease using an Assignment and Assumption Agreement) and will have a new stock certificate issued to them in their name.

The purchaser signs all of the loan documents, verifying the interest rate, the lender's security interest in the shares and leases, and the payment terms. The lender's attorney should bring checks for the net proceeds of the purchaser's loan to the closing, allocated according to the instructions of the buyer's attorney. The seller must bring all copies of the keys, including mailbox and building entrance door keys, to be exchanged with the transfer documents and purchase payment.

In some states, there is no personal meeting at an attorney's office or physical exchange of documents or funds. Instead, all the funds are transferred through a settlement or escrow agent's office. These are frequently distributed before the actual closing day, usually via wire or bank check(s), with documents being executed in advance.

Not knowing about the closing ahead of time is a cause of anxiety for many people. Becoming familiar with the *closing road map* prior to embarking on your journey to owning your own home will allow you to enjoy a (relatively) stress-free experience.

CHAPTER SUMMARY AND INSIDER TIPS

- Do not trust appraisers in determining what amount you should pay for a home. Trust yourself after visiting numerous properties. Consult your broker as well, but remember that he or she has an interest in your paying a higher amount due to the nature of commissions.
- Never sign documents without having an attorney look them over first.
- Always make sure you have the seller's forwarding address and cell phone number. This information is for any post-closing questions or issues that arise. For example, the seller may have left behind a wonderful alarm system that you need information on how to work.
- Remember the phrase *Caveat Emptor—Let the Buyer Beware*. You are buying the home as is—so once you have closed and received the keys, the seller is no longer liable for any repairs (except in some states).
- Most closings do not occur on the date written in the contract of sale, since this is merely an estimated date. The process of getting everything and everyone—the buyer, seller, lender, title company, both attorneys—together becomes an event in itself. Other factors that might potentially cause delay include requirements from the lender, the seller's need to move into a new home, and countless other issues that may arise. In fact, it's quite rare to obtain a closing date before or on the listed date.
- You do not have a deal or a binding contract until both the seller and the buyer sign. No judge will award you the home based on a handshake and an oral promise.
- Make an effort to negotiate clauses and contingencies that will protect you. Ensure that your contract includes a mortgage contingency clause, in addition to one that allows you to cancel the transaction if the property appraises beneath the purchase price.

Chapter 13 Using the Home Inspection to Lower the Price

Similar in purpose to a routine physical examination performed by a medical doctor to determine a person's health, the goal of a home inspection is to determine the physical condition of the home. Potential homebuyers should be aware of the physical condition of their investment as well as the need for and cost of repairs, if any, necessary for the home to be livable. Since any potential major repair cost could significantly drive down the selling price of the home, the home inspection could result in a reduction or renegotiation of the purchase price to deduct the replacement or repair costs of any substandard items.

Even bargain hunters seeking to put their own sweat and equity into a fixer-upper benefit from knowledge of the home's repair needs and whether they could exceed the buyer's own capabilities. As long as you are aware that you are purchasing a home that requires repairs, and are paying a price that has been reduced by the amount needed to perform the repairs after closing, a home in need of repairs could potentially provide a good opportunity for buying at a discount.

A home inspection should inform prospective buyers of the property systems' life expectancy, maintenance needs, and functions. Overall, an inspector should be skilled at determining whether any problems are lurking beyond the scope of a homebuyer's untrained eyes. For that reason, you want to schedule the home inspector's visit immediately upon oral agreement on purchase terms.

THE INSPECTION

A typical home inspection takes from one to three hours, depending on the dwelling's size and idiosyncrasies. Equipped with sophisticated engineering tools as well as common implements such as flashlights, electrical testers, carbon monoxide and fuel gas detectors, moisture meters, ladders and inspection mirrors, the home inspector will examine the premises.

Among the systems that the inspector must examine, at a minimum, are the basic support structures, the plumbing, heating, air conditioning and electrical systems. A more thorough inspection checks for faulty electrical wiring, electrical systems' effectiveness, and whether galvanized steel exists and its efficacy. It also includes checking water supply pipes, looking for underground oil tanks, wells, and/or septic systems, and detecting any mold and/or leaks. The water pressure should also be measured and the water tested for bacteria. Drainage systems should be tested and, in certain locations, the air in the house should be tested for radon gas and paint tested for lead if the home was built before 1978. The insulation, wood framing, doors, and windows should be examined for defects, and the premises should be checked for wood destroying insects. Furthermore, items that may contain asbestos should be scrutinized and tested; however, do not assume that all asbestos is dangerous. Only that which can become airborne in an enclosed environment presents a hazard.

The inspector must also assess whether alterations and additions have been completed properly, and alert the buyer to find out whether the proper permits and certificate of occupancy or certificate of completion have been obtained.

Focus areas for home inspectors can vary with region. For example, important inspection points in California include checking for previous earthquake damage and for signs of structural damage to the foundation of the property.

Attending the Inspection and Obtaining a Written Report

As the buyer, you should be present for the inspection if possible. This will not only allow you to learn about your future home's condition and how its systems function; you'll also become aware of major appliances' remaining life span and any potential problems lurking around the home. The inspector should give you an oral diagnosis at the time of the inspection and follow up with a detailed written report soon thereafter. Any safety issues should be discussed, as well as the other positive and negative features of the dwelling. Many inspectors may give you estimates on the cost of repairing mentioned defects. Although sometimes unfettered access may not be available, the buyer would nevertheless be wise to obtain cost estimates from reputable independent contractors for any repairs or replacements.

Inspection of Multi-Family Dwellings

In addition to the above referenced items, a review of multi-family dwellings should include, but not be limited to, inspection of the elevator, drains, oil storage tanks or underground tanks, services for gas, oil, and water, entrances and exits, as well as the individual unit or units involved in the purchase. The roof, roof materials, parapet walls, flashings, safety, and ventilation should be analyzed. Inspectors of multi-family units may also examine heat delivery systems, warping, water damage, the electrical panel and outlets, front door security, and carbon monoxide and smoke detectors, in addition to other fire safety considerations.

Cooperative and Condominium Purchases

When purchasing a unit in a cooperative or condominium building, most buyers fail to secure a home inspection. If you are not going to order a report, then be sure to carefully review the written reports of the board of directors' (manager's) meetings for the previous two years and determine the amount in the reserve fund. This should reveal most major building problems, and whether the building can afford to pay for repairs while remaining economically secure. However, when the data is sparse or when buyers want to carefully protect their investment, a proper inspection of the unit and the common elements of the building should be obtained.

FINDING THE RIGHT HOME INSPECTOR

The Timing

You should seek references for a home inspector as soon as you are coming close to making an offer for a property. For properties with multiple bidders—or when a cancellation period in a contract of sale cannot be negotiated—an immediate inspection will be necessary to avoid endangering the deal. In most states, the buyer purchases an existing home in as is condition or Let the Buyer Beware. Absent fraud, in most cases, a buyer will usually have no remedy if there were to be a problem once the closing occurs and the deed is delivered.

Referrals and Licensing

Seek referrals only from people who have experienced a satisfactory home inspection or who are intimately involved in the buying or selling of homes, such as real estate attorneys and other real estate professionals. Be wary of any person who has an interest in the sale of the property, such as the seller or a broker who is earning a commission. Inspectors being referred business may have dual loyalty, and may therefore be biased toward approving the condition of the home to help persons contributing to their income. Once you have collected at least three names of recommended home inspectors, you should begin interviewing and calling to get an appointment with one of them.

Since some states require the inspector to hold a license, confirm whether yours does. Inquire as well about the number of homes with which the prospective inspector has worked that are similar to your impending purchase. For example, a New York City inspector may not be the best choice for a Westchester property, where an expertise in termites and oil tanks is necessary. Equally, the Westchester inspector may not be knowledgeable about the elevator examinations necessary for some inspections of Manhattan properties. Take care to hire the *inspector* and not the company's name, and confirm that the individual who inspected your referral sources' homes is the same person who will be doing your inspection. Alternatively, ensure that you are satisfied with the credentials of the inspector. Choosing a home inspector licensed in engineering may enhance the visit. Every state regulates the practice of engineering, but not as many states require licenses for home inspectors.

The Price

In much of the nation, a home inspection costs anywhere between $350 and $2,500, depending on the property's size and location. Determine whether the price includes a detailed written report that supplies the answers to questions and concerns. Also determine whether the inspector will be available for follow-up questions after you receive the written report and whether they will give estimates of the costs of the required repairs.

QUICK INSIDER TIP

Learning from Other Buyers' Nightmares

Although typical home inspections won't uncover the haunted house type of problems that inspired movies like *Poltergeist* (ghosts in homes built on a former graveyard) and *Amityville Horror* (house haunted by angry former resident), most significant problems can and should be found during a good and thorough inspection.

At the turn of the millennium, one of the largest and most reputable inspection companies gave a glowing inspection report to a multi-unit dwelling in New York. No more than two months after closing, it became public that there was serious structural damage, which had not only existed prior to the inspection, it actually warranted the demolition of the entire building.

In another case, a homebuyer hired a local engineer recommended by their real estate agent to inspect the property. This recommended

(*continued*)

(continued)
inspector not only failed to discover an active oil tank that protruded into the backyard, but also failed to detect that it was leaking. Half of the house, including the entire basement and main level bathrooms, had to be gutted and replaced. With the buyer lacking proper insurance, experts and lawyers spent thousands and thousands of dollars of this family's money to try to rectify the situation, and as of this date no end to this debacle is in sight. The family has moved to another home and is carrying two mortgages, while the oil tank is being exhumed and the property sits on the market for sale.

Finally, a further example to illustrate the importance of conducting a proper inspection: Using a large inspection company in New Jersey, one condominium unit buyer learned after an inspection and closing that the heating system in his home was missing. The inspection company refused to reimburse any of the costs to the buyer despite the fact that they acknowledged the mistake. (Please see *My Story: The Walk Through*, in Chapter 15, to learn more about this situation.)

Of course, all of these scenarios could have been avoided had a reputable company willing to stand behind its work performed a capable and thorough inspection. It is my hope that these horror stories will persuade the reader to be extremely careful about this step in the home buying process, and to follow the guidelines that I have outlined in order to prevent similar avoidable catastrophes.

PROTECTING YOURSELF WHEN SIGNING THE CONTRACT OF SALE

If the inspection has not occurred by the date the contract of sale is ready to be signed, it is important that a clause be added to the contract permitting the buyer not only a certain small number of days to conduct an inspection, but also the option to cancel the contract if structural damage or repair work in excess of a set maximum amount is present. Alternatively, the contract may require the seller to pay for or fix any repairs reported before the closing date with a maximum amount, after which the seller would have the option to cancel the contract and refund the buyer's down payment. Depending on market conditions, the seller may agree in the contract of sale to pay for any damage up to a certain monetary amount, or even to permit the buyer to cancel the contract of sale. However, many sellers, particularly in an overheated market, will not tolerate such an amendment to the contract of sale and may choose to sell to a less fastidious purchaser instead.

Other important additions to the contract include representations of sale: that the plumbing, heating, and electrical systems are in working order, and that the roof and basement are free of leaks and will be in working order at the time of closing. Even when a seller does not agree to these suggested clauses, some states—New York, for example—require sellers to complete a detailed 48-item questionnaire called the Property Condition Disclosure Act (PCDA), to be delivered to the buyer before the contract is signed. However, according to New York law, if the seller does not complete or deliver a PCDA, then the only detriment to the seller is crediting the purchaser with $500 at closing.

The purpose of the home inspection is to protect your investment in your home, and to give you the opportunity to learn more about your property's internal and external mechanisms. Most importantly, it brings you one step closer to a safe and informed home buying experience.

CHAPTER SUMMARY AND INSIDER TIPS

- Always accompany the inspector when visiting the home. You will learn about your home and its structure, as well as important information about the lifespan of its systems and major components.
- Ask for referrals. The inspector is doing an x-ray and diagnosis of your house. Just as you would not pick a heart surgeon from a phonebook, be sure to ask for referrals when hiring a home inspector—but only from people who have experienced a satisfactory home inspection or who are intimately involved in the home buying or selling process.
- Cross out waivers and any limitation of liability when signing a contract with an inspector or engineer. Your inspector should be held responsible for missing any major repair items in the inspection.
- Spend money to have the inspector accompany you during the pre-closing walk through. This will be your last chance to identify repair issues before you're stuck with paying for them yourself. Make sure that all facilities that were working when you first visited the home are still working at the time of closing. If not, make sure you delay the closing or obtain credits for the costs of remedying these situations.
- Send the inspector to the home as soon as you have an accepted offer. Unless the sale contract will be contingent on the inspection, you may lose the chance to buy the home if it takes too long for you to sign the contract because you're waiting for the inspector.

Chapter 14 Finding, Hiring, and Utilizing an Aggressive Attorney

Countless consumers spend hours combing through stores for the perfect outfit and the cheapest sale price for a piece of clothing. However, when it comes to selecting an attorney for what may be the most significant investment of their lifetime—the purchase or sale of real estate—they will often make random and hasty selections. This is frequently due to the buyer or seller's lack of experience and expertise in the process; after all, very few people buy and sell homes on a routine basis. This chapter will attempt to educate buyers on how to find, hire, and utilize the best possible attorney to represent them in this incredibly important transaction.

WARNING: A number of states, including Nevada and California for smaller property transactions, do not involve attorneys in the purchase or sale of property. This is a huge mistake in my opinion; I firmly believe that the practice in these states should be changed. I have litigated cases where people have lost their life savings and homes as a result of the failure to use an attorney or the proper attorney. I hope that reading this chapter will help convince readers to hire an attorney.

WHETHER TO HIRE AN ATTORNEY

Although not required by law, buyers and sellers in many states hire an attorney when purchasing or selling property. Every year, huge numbers of cases are litigated across the nation involving a real estate transaction gone wrong. In most, the cause was the failure of one or both parties to hire an attorney qualified to handle the transaction or to hire an attorney at all. In most of these cases, the mistake, misunderstanding, or fraud resulting in the litigation most likely could have been prevented by using an experienced attorney.

Some examples of transactions gone wrong involve the failure of the purchaser or seller to catch a problem, whether it involves the failure to transfer the entire property contracted, or fraud, theft, hidden oil tanks, property line disputes, lead paint disclosures, failure to meet loan contingency deadlines, or undisclosed conditions or history of the property.

Many litigated claims are unavoidable. However, gambling with one of the most important investments of a lifetime is not advisable, and this risk can be minimized by retaining a good attorney. Although most deals do close without litigation, it is wiser to save all gambling for a casino.

FINDING AN ATTORNEY

Put away the yellow pages and forego Internet searches! Buyers should speak to people they trust who have purchased previously and ask them for references to an experienced real estate attorney. When asking for references, be sure to ask specific questions and listen to why these people were satisfied with their attorneys. Ask them to give you the best and the worst qualities possessed by the attorney.

Any members of the real estate industry whom you know are also a great source of information. Fellow attorneys are usually good at evaluating their peers, and most real estate professionals—including home inspectors, lending officers, and others who repeatedly work with real estate attorneys—should provide adequate guidance. Although persons in the industry can be extremely informative and helpful, almost anyone who has purchased a property is a good source for recommendations. However, be careful to ask yourself if the person making the recommendation has anything to gain from their referral when evaluating any suggestion.

THE MINI-INTERVIEW

This is when it's time to run an Internet search in order to gather information and call the referenced attorney. The attorney should provide you with free advice on the closing process during your first call or mini-interview, and may even be willing to address some questions or concerns involving your specific transaction. This interaction will not only give you the chance to get some helpful information, but will also show you whether this attorney may be the right person for the job.

QUESTIONS FOR THE ATTORNEY CANDIDATE(S)

Asking attorneys to describe their experiences with transactions similar to yours will give you the opportunity to gauge their level of expertise. Whether or not this individual promptly—and by that I mean within 24 hours—returns your phone call is another important factor to consider. The number one complaint that clients have about their lawyers is the lawyers' failure to return phone calls.

You may want to ask how many closings the attorney has completed involving the type of property you are purchasing. Many who have done hundreds of residential home closings may have never represented purchasers in buying cooperative apartments, a condominium, a vacant lot, or a farm. For example, a crucial deciding factor in determining whether to consummate the purchase of a condominium apartment comes from an in-depth and accurate understanding of the condominium's financial statements, the contents of its offering plan, and more specifically, its declaration, bylaws, proprietary lease, and house rules and regulations. A competent attorney for such a transaction will be able to discuss with a client the economic stability of the condominium and the rules and regulations governing the building by reviewing the condominium's documents, the offering plan, and any amendments. This is even more important in the event you are purchasing a cooperative apartment.

For larger law firms, clients should question who will be representing them during the transaction and attending the real estate closing. Though the referred attorney will often oversee the deal in bigger firms, he or she does not directly participate in the negotiating or closing process, or may work with another attorney or staff member on the deal. You should ask for clarification as to how involved your attorney and other staff members will be. If other staff members have substantial input, you should speak with them to make sure that you are as confident and comfortable with the other members of the closing team as with the lead attorney.

WHEN TO CONSULT AN ATTORNEY

You want to consult an attorney as soon as you start looking to purchase a property. You should allow yourself enough time to find the right one; when done well, this will allow you to facilitate the purchase process and improve your chance of obtaining the property you desire.

You should ask the attorney to tell you the fee, and whether it will be fixed or hourly. If fixed, what services are included in the fee and what would be additional? If hourly, what are the rates for the people involved, and what is the estimated total fee? Ask for a written engagement letter which explains all that.

Your attorney should know that you are looking for a place to live before you even decide to make an offer on a specific property. You'll want to disclose your basic requirements and any unusual circumstances. At the outset, you can obtain basic advice from your attorney, and many attorneys may even recommend other professionals including mortgage and real estate brokers, banks, and home inspectors to assist you.

Finding your attorney early in the process puts you in a position to trump other bidders, since you can have your attorney start working on the deal while other bidders are still scrambling to find an attorney. Since you are starting early in the process you will have adequate time to scout and find the right attorney for you and your transaction.

THE FUNCTIONS OF THE PURCHASER'S ATTORNEY

A good purchaser's attorney advocates and protects a client's interests when participating in a real estate transaction. Discuss the terms of your offer with your attorney. Also, check whether you need to make the contract contingent on obtaining financing. Once the seller accepts your offer and the contract of sale is prepared, your attorney will review and negotiate its terms. In some areas, the seller's attorney normally prepares the contract of sale and then sends it to the buyer's attorney. The buyer's attorney would then review the contract, go over any necessary points with the buyer, and negotiate changes as necessary.

In other areas, the real estate broker usually prepares the contract and sometimes signs before the buyer's attorney reviews it. The buyer's attorney then has a limited number of days to accept the contract as it is written or to disapprove the contract and negotiate changes to protect the buyer. In many such locations, the buyers' attorneys routinely issue disapprovals, rendering brokers' contracts almost meaningless.

When purchasing a condominium or a cooperative apartment, the purchaser's attorney has an obligation to review all organizational documents related to the building, including the proprietary lease, its amendments, the bylaws, and the house rules. Since the seller is leaving the building, the seller is less interested in the governing documents, except those portions relating to any transfer fees such as move out fees and *flip taxes*. However, prudent sellers will want to have these documents on hand to furnish to the buyer. The documents will dictate many rules governing living in the building, including whether pets are permitted, whether a transfer fee is applied on the sale of a unit, and how the building is managed.

The attorney should also review the minutes of the meetings of the co-op corporation's board of managers/directors over the last two years. These recorded minutes are required by law and provide a written record of important matters discussed concerning the building. Many times these minutes will flag important problems affecting the financial or structural integrity of the building. In the case of a cooperative apartment, since you are buying shares (and not land) in a cooperative corporation, it is crucial that the financial statements of the cooperative for at least two years are analyzed to ensure its financial stability. Many purchasers' attorneys also send a questionnaire to the building's managing agent to solicit other information relating to the viability of the building, including recent capital improvements, anticipated future improvements or major repairs, and anticipated means of financing for such work or repairs. If you are purchasing a building that was previously an ordinary rental, your attorney will also want to know what percentage of the building is owner-occupied.

If you're purchasing a cooperative apartment, your attorney will order a lien search to ensure that no encumbrances or liens impair the unit. A lien search serves the same function as a title search: It determines whether there are any judgments or liens against the seller or the building. Any such judgments against the seller will have to be removed prior to or at the closing in order for you to receive clean title to the shares. If there are judgments against the entire building in a co-op, you and your lender should obtain the details and information about how they'll have to be paid.

When purchasing a condominium or a house, the buyer's attorney orders and reviews a title report, which is a summary of the current state of the seller's title to the property. The buyer's attorney will then investigate whether there are any liens, mortgages, or judgments against the property or the seller, confirm that the seller owns the property, check on the status of taxes, request an update of an existing survey, and look over the engineer's or home inspection report.

The attorney will thoroughly review the title report and survey and ensure that you're purchasing the home free of any title defects raised in the report. Your lawyer should also explain to you the various options you may or may not have with regard to title insurance. While there remain many localities throughout the nation where title insurance is commonly seen as an expensive luxury, this is a tragic fiction. You should regard title insurance as an absolute must.

The attorney should also review all important literature, such as all documents from the lending institution (including your commitment letter). He or she should advise you of all closing costs including any taxes owed and financing costs. Unfortunately, when financing is involved, your attorney usually cannot give you the exact closing costs until he receives the amounts from the lender's attorneys.

Another area of concern, particularly in single family homes, is whether any changes or improvements have been made to the property without obtaining the proper permits or sign-offs. The creation of decks, swimming pools, additional rooms, or dwelling spaces are frequent issues.

If you're buying a multi-family dwelling like a two-, three- or four-family house, your attorney should be active in conducting an extensive process of due diligence. Depending on the property's location, this process might entail an investigation into whether rent regulation affects the building's purchase; whether there are legal limits and procedures regarding rent, utilities, water charges, security deposits, zoning; and other regulatory issues. As with any purchase, the building should undergo a comprehensive inspection.

After the contract is negotiated and signed and the down payment is sent to the seller's attorney, the buyer's attorney will review any relevant documents concerning obtaining financing from a lender. The attorney also prepares/reviews all relevant closing documents to ensure that a proper title is transferred. These may include but are not limited to the survey and the title insurance policy if applicable.

Once the closing date approaches, the attorney will notify everyone who must attend the closing and collect any documents that the lender, title company, or managing agent require. In addition to obtaining copies of all the closing documents, do not forget to get the keys, any alarm codes, instructions, warranties, garage door openers, and a letter to the doorman and move-in instructions for multi-family buildings.

THE MAKINGS OF A GOOD REAL ESTATE ATTORNEY

As previously mentioned, a good real estate attorney will always return clients' calls and e-mails within 24 hours. Attorneys should hold their clients' hands through the entire process and answer all questions eagerly. As the client, you should be apprised of all developments, and your attorney should continue to educate you on each process and its significance during the transaction. He or she should thoroughly explain the contract's content to you. In the case of the purchase of a cooperative apartment, it is the attorney's duty to prepare you for the board interview. Before the closing, the client should understand the financial implications of the purchase and be aware of the precise amounts due to the different entities involved and how they must be paid. Most sums payable at the closing are required to be paid by certified or bank check.

After the closing, the client should receive a closing statement detailing the transaction and the flow of money, as well as a copy of every document signed at closing. These documents should be retained in a safe place for as long as possible but at least until a future sale.

By understanding the role of the attorney as well as the transfer process, buyers will be better able to protect themselves and facilitate a stress-free transaction.

CHAPTER SUMMARY AND INSIDER TIPS

- Leave ample time to find the right attorney for your purchase—and most definitely use an attorney. You can start searching for one as soon as you decide to buy. By deciding upon an attorney early on in the process, you will be ahead of competing buyers who still need to do so before negotiating terms and closing the deal.

- Do not use the phonebook or the Internet in your search. Instead, ask people you trust for references and referrals for a good real estate attorney. The most useful people from whom to request these recommendations are those who recently purchased property and were happy with their attorney. Real estate industry professionals such as brokers, home inspectors, and lending professionals can also be great sources for this type of information. However, be on the alert if any of these referring sources appear to be too cozy with the attorney. Remember that they might have something to gain from suggesting this attorney, and that they might not be giving completely objective advice.

- Don't just obtain a name for your referrals; ask those making the referrals to also evaluate these individuals' performances and give you both the positives and the negatives of their experience.

- Once you have gotten names for some potential candidates, take the time to conduct some Internet research to see what you can learn about them. However, do not let your Internet findings alone guide you; make sure that you call any attorneys whom you are seriously considering and actually speak to these people themselves.

- When speaking to a potential attorney candidate, discern whether he or she has experience representing buyers in purchases involving the same type of property that you are trying to buy. Each type of property brings its own special considerations and nuances to the purchase process. To that end, it is important for your attorney to be familiar with all the steps involved in your particular type of transaction so that you aren't at a disadvantage.

- Once you have selected an attorney who is knowledgeable and experienced in the type of purchase you want to make and whom you feel you can trust with this important transaction, you can also consult him or her to find other real estate professionals whom you'll need to refer to at various stages during the purchase process, including brokers, home inspectors, and lending professionals

Chapter 15 The Walk Through
The Final Inspection

Real estate professionals use the term *walk through* for the final inspection, which usually occurs approximately 24 hours before the closing date. Unfortunately, too many buyers spend more time buying a t-shirt or choosing a brand of shampoo than investigating whether a home's components are in working order. Because buying a home is such an important transaction, a careful review or inspection of the premises should be conducted shortly before closing.

THE WALK THROUGH AS AN INSPECTION

A buyer should treat the walk through as an inspection. Many real estate purchasers bring along persons handy with repairs when they do a walk through. These competent persons should test everything that can possibly be tested. All appliances and systems should be inspected and turned on. All doors and cabinets should be opened, rugs and furniture moved, and all hidden spots scrutinized. For newly constructed properties, consider hiring an engineer to do a final complete inspection of the home and all its major components.

THE PUNCH LIST

Make a list of items that have possibly broken or been removed between the initial inspection and closing, as well as items that are not in working order in accordance with the contract of sale. The itemized list prepared for closing is usually called the *punch list*. Before the closing, get ballpark estimates of the cost of repairs and/or replacements. At many closings, buyers will want the items on the punch list corrected by the seller, or the buyer may seek a credit at the closing for the costs of the items' repair or their replacement value. For expensive or vital items, the closing may have to be adjourned until the problem is taken care of and repairs completed, but any such action should take into account the impact of the delay on your mortgage commitment if you opt for a postponement. The punch list and walk through supplement the inspection that should have been completed upon, before, or shortly after signing the contract of sale.

Most contracts require that all appliances, heating units, and air conditioning systems are in working order, and that the roof and basement are free of leaks upon closing. Contracts may also include other seller representations as to the condition of the unit.

LET THE BUYER BEWARE

Many times, real estate purchasers conduct a run through rather than a walk through—meaning that they miss items that they should never miss. For example, one buyer of a newly constructed property somehow failed to notice that her ceiling was built a few feet lower than promised, while another client didn't detect that the floors had a tilt so huge that one could roll a ball across the floor without applying any physical exertion. Yet another client closed without realizing that his heating system was nonexistent (an example I discuss further in *My Story: The Walk Through*).

Do not forget that your contract dictates that you are buying the home as is (which does not always apply in the case of a newly constructed home). Once you have the keys—and if the item is not on the punch list, or hasn't been cited in a contract amendment—do not expect the seller to answer your calls if you find that further repairs are needed. Unless otherwise stated, the seller's obligation to fix problems ends once the closing takes place and the deed has been delivered.

When single family homes are involved, some states, such as New York, require sellers to list all of the defects in a property disclosure questionnaire, as prescribed by the Property Condition Disclosure Act (PCDA). However, the only result is that the seller must issue a $500 credit to the buyer if the seller does not furnish the PCDA. This extensive questionnaire covers so many topics that most attorneys recommend that sellers do not even contemplate delivering one. I therefore usually suggest to sellers that they always agree to issue the credit so they will not be liable for any repairs and problems after the closing occurs. Once the credit is issued—unless flagrant fraud is involved—the buyer will be responsible for anything that needs to be fixed post-closing. This is another reason that buyers need to be vigilant during the walk through.

In many states, including New York, newly constructed homes have special laws protecting buyers beyond the closing date. However, getting a developer to abide by these laws can take years and cost an inordinate amount in legal fees.

MY STORY: THE WALK THROUGH

Shortly after striking out on my own as a lawyer, one of my closest friends and housemates at Rutgers College, Mark, asked me to represent him in purchasing a home. Honored that he trusted me with the largest investment of his life, I channeled all of my passion into attempting to provide him with the greatest legal representation possible. Part of my fervor in trying to impress Mark came from the hours he had spent teaching me the lessons he had learned from his father on how to save money. Naturally, I was anxious to help Mark and to demonstrate my own expertise. In college, I frequently referred to Mark as my financial advisor, and we would practice the lessons he taught me together. This was my chance to pay back the favor.

One of these lessons was self-imposed. Since we lived on an extremely small budget, we ate at least one meal a day, usually dinner, at a local place called M V Deli located about 100 yards from our house. I fell in
(continued)

(*continued*)

love with their roast beef and turkey sandwiches, not only because they were bigger than 12 inches and full of meat, but also because the entire hero cost only $3.25, by far the best deal in town. Unfortunately, I ate these sandwiches so often that it took me another 15 years after college before I could even contemplate downing another turkey sandwich.

I knew that Mark would find the best deal in town, since no one knew how to find a bargain better than he did. He searched and searched, and finally found his dream home: a duplex in mint condition in Fort Lee, New Jersey. He needed me to close the deal, and in spite of my best intentions, I regrettably wound up failing him in one vital component of the transaction.

At the end of Mark's closing, we started celebrating the purchase; we even gave each other high fives as we walked outside my office. Mark was proud to be a homeowner and I was proud to be his lawyer. He took me out to eat. Everything gleamed. But, as it turned out, we were declaring victory too soon.

A few months later after the weather turned cold, Mark called to let me know that the heat in his home was not working. He learned that the brand new heat pump the seller had boasted about purchasing to help close the sale did not include the piece necessary for proper heating—only air conditioning. The home inspector he had used—whom I had recommended to him—would not return his calls, and neither would the seller. Although Mark did a walk through of the apartment, he never thought to check to see if the heating system was working or even if it existed. After all, the sale took place during the summer; the unit was brand new, and the air conditioning was working fine. Since he had hired a professional inspector and the sellers seemed like nice people, he thought he was protected. After speaking to the heat pump's installer, he learned the seller had refused to spend the extra couple of hundred dollars to purchase a proper unit, which would have contained the proper heating component.

Of course, mistakes happen; so I figured a call from me to the inspection company's owner would rectify the situation. I assumed that the inspector would do the right thing and pay for a new heating system. However, he offered me nothing except the advice that "I should sue him," citing the fine print in the report Mark received, disclaiming any liability. Although I wrote letters and continued to call, it was all to no avail.

I had received the name of this inspector from another deal I had done in New Jersey. Foolishly, I never checked the references. Looking back, it is clear that I had relied too heavily on my referral source for such an important assignment.

Aside from all of that, however, it was also my fault for failing to instruct Mark on how to conduct a proper walk through to make sure everything was working as it should. I should have emphasized that regardless of home inspectors or the integrity of sellers, buyers must still play an active role in the walk through in order to protect their own interests. I offered to assist him in suing the seller and the inspector in small claims court for free. However, Mark declined, noting that a replacement system cost about $2,500 and he did not want to waste my time nor any more of his money in court.

From this sorry experience, we both learned valuable yet costly lessons. And both of us continue to strive to live within our means.

CHAPTER SUMMARY AND INSIDER TIPS

- Purchasing property is likely to be one of the most significant financial transactions of your life. For that reason, you must not underestimate the importance of conducting a thorough walk through before closing.
- Treat the walk through as a final inspection. If you strive for ultimate perfection or if an engineer found problems during the initial inspection, you can hire an inspector to accompany you for the walk through. Otherwise, try to bring people who are knowledgeable and skillful in home repairs. If you cannot find such persons to accompany you, make sure you at least bring a friend. Do not underestimate the value of another pair of eyes when taking this vital step in the process.
- Allow ample time to conduct the walk through; you want to be able to test everything that can possibly be tested. Examine every aspect of the property with a keen eye and attention to detail. Turn on every appliance, faucet, and light switch. Open each door and cabinet. Move rugs and furniture to scrutinize hidden spots. Do not forget to examine your outdoor land and fixtures too.
- Be thorough in your punch list. Cite anything that has broken or deteriorated between the initial inspection and the walk through, and bring this list to the seller's attention at closing.
- You can seek to have the items on the punch list repaired or replaced, or you can ask the seller for a credit at closing if these items fail to meet the standard stipulated in the contract of sale. For serious problems, you may adjourn the closing until the problem is completely resolved.

Chapter 16 The Importance of Homeowner's Insurance

Acquiring the Knowledge to Purchase and Maintain a Sufficient Policy for Your Home or Investment Property

In this age of both natural and unnatural disasters, Americans have a newfound desire for security. As a result, few debate the importance of homeowner's insurance. Yet despite this fact, many homes are either underinsured or improperly insured. To paraphrase Franklin D. Roosevelt's famous thought, it is in the unknown where fear should lie. Property owners need their insurance policies to provide adequate coverage both for any damage to the property itself and for liability to other people under circumstances involving the property.

Although traditional banks require a borrower to purchase homeowner's insurance, lenders usually don't provide too many details on these policies' limitations. This chapter's goal is to keep you from becoming a shocked and angry underinsured homeowner by teaching you some of the basic ins and outs of homeowner's insurance policies.

THE HOMEOWNER'S INSURANCE POLICY

A homeowner's policy includes two types of insurance: property insurance, which insures the house itself against perils such as fire, and liability insurance, which insures the homeowner against liability to other persons, such as guests who are injured on the property. Although both of these types of insurance are contained in a homeowner's policy, there are various versions of such a policy.

Homeowner's policies follow what are called the ISO (Insurance Services Office) forms. The HO1 is the basic, plain vanilla policy. The HO2 covers more perils (events that may cause a loss). The HO3 is the typical single family home policy—an *all risk* policy with just a few perils excluded. The HO5 is *Cadillac coverage*—it covers even more than the HO3. Homeowner's insurance is paid annually, with an average cost of about $765 per year nationwide (according to the Regulatory Research Corporation).

THE FUNCTION OF THE HOMEOWNER'S INSURANCE POLICY

Although insurance policies may differ slightly depending on the state where the property is located, the various types are relatively standard. The standard policy should provide coverage for your home's structure and contents in the event of a disaster or theft, and also allow an ample amount to pay the legal claims of anyone hurt in your home. The standard policy should also provide coverage for your living costs should you be required to vacate your home due to a disaster that the policy covers.

Although you'll receive the option to only insure the value of the structures and possessions you lose, it is far wiser to pay the higher premium, which enables you to replace them with new, comparable items. A homeowner can purchase either an ACV (Actual Cash Value) policy, which is the norm; a Replacement Cost policy—which will replace the loss without regard to depreciation—for an extra premium; or a Guaranteed Replacement Cost policy, which will replace the property regardless of the policy limits.

Homeowner's insurance policies do not cover general maintenance-related issues, and you should not assume that your policy takes care of every possible type of disaster or damage. For example, some standard policies cover terrorist attacks but not acts of war. Do not assume that your safety can be measured by your distance from this nation's coastlines; after all, one of the most notorious attacks in our country's history took place in Oklahoma City. Many standard policies also exclude flood, earthquake, and lead paint casualties, although coverage for these can usually be purchased at an additional cost.

It bears reemphasizing that the standard policy does not pay for the replacement cost of damaged or lost items. Standard insurance only covers the value of the item at the time of the incident—the item's cost less deprecation—which value is usually far less than you think it will be. A more expensive replacement cost policy can be purchased to better insure the owner.

Another common misconception is that the policy will insure the value of the house including any appreciation. In this instance, you must request to add extra coverage to your policy.

It should be noted that your liability insurance coverage is limited to the amount of the policy unless additional protections have been purchased, such as an umbrella policy that provides additional liability insurance. In my opinion, every homeowner ought to have a PLUP (Personal Liability Umbrella Policy). Such policies are very cheap compared to other types of insurance. Verdicts awarded to plaintiffs by juries today can be astronomical, and it is very comforting to have a $3,000,000 umbrella over a $1,000,000 primary policy.

WAYS TO REDUCE THE COST OF HOMEOWNER'S INSURANCE

You can select a policy with higher deductibles in order to substantially reduce insurance costs. Alternatively, insurance companies may provide you with a reduced premium if you use the same company to purchase your home and auto insurance policies. You can also cut down on this cost by citing factors like your proximity to a fire hydrant and/or fire station. Shop around for your homeowner's insurance policy, and be sure to ask company representatives about current discounts and promotions and whether your personal circumstances qualify you for a discount. For instance, people above a certain age will qualify for a discount in many states.

MAINTAINING A HOMEOWNER'S INSURANCE POLICY

In case an incident or disaster occurs, homeowners should be prepared to prove to the insurer the totality of their destroyed personal property and belongings. Therefore, you'll want to make a proper list all of the personal items in your home long before you have a problem. You can supplement this inventory list with a video recording or pictures of the insured property. Save receipts and credit card statements for this purpose, and constantly update this to include new purchases. Since you're preparing for the total or partial loss of your home, you'll want to make a copy of this inventory somewhere else. You could write it out in an e-mail and periodically send it to yourself and one other person. Also, you should notify the insurance company of any important or sizable purchases, such as jewelry. You may need to buy *insurance riders* to increase the amount of your insurance policy accordingly. It should be noted that most insurance companies insure the loss of your property even when it is stolen or lost in a place other than your home. Some insurance companies cover luggage lost overseas in their standard policy. Check with your agent to see if this is the case.

Inform your insurance company in writing about any major improvements to your home, and request them to add coverage to the policy. You should document improvements, not just for insurance purposes, but because they affect your tax basis if and when you sell. This may require you to order an appraisal or have the insurance company do one to make sure you have insured the property adequately.

The standard homeowner's policy will even protect you to some extent if you are sued. In this case, the policy takes on the risk of any legal costs incurred, including judgments and legal fees. However, there are two important numbers to look out for in this situation: the deductible and the limits. If your deductible is too high or your limits are too low, a relatively simple lawsuit can bring about financial ruin and force you to forfeit your house. On the other hand, you do not want to cripple yourself with premiums. You should therefore carefully consider carrying this cost when you are deciding how expensive a home and policy to buy. To avoid losing potential insurance proceeds, you should also be aware of any notice or time requirements for reporting a problem or loss. In addition, you want to document any harm immediately after the occurrence, preferably with both narrative and photographs.

INSURANCE THROUGH THE FEDERAL GOVERNMENT

Other important but little-known resources are policies provided by state and federal governments that may step in when the insurance companies bow out. For example, the Federal Government National Flood Insurance Program provides flood insurance to homeowners. Even though they are supplied by the government, such insurances can be purchased through your insurance agent. You should ask what kinds of insurance your state offers.

HOMEOWNER'S INSURANCE IN COOPERATIVES AND CONDOMINIUMS

For cooperative shareholders and condominium unit owners, the management usually maintains a master policy for the structure and common areas of the building. However, you'll need to obtain a separate policy for each individual unit and its contents. A wise purchaser will determine whether the cooperative or condominium's master policy sufficiently protects the building. A copy of the master policy should be provided to your insurance company to determine the amount of additional protection needed for your unit. As a young attorney, I never forgot the teachings of a top real estate attorney, who recommended that a shareholder should buy insurance from the same company that the cooperative board insures the building with. He reasoned that this would prevent possible conflicts in case the insurance companies disagree on which policy covers a particular mishap.

Consider this example: a unit owner, having water damage in her unit, claims the damage is caused by the pipes inside the wall or from the neighbor's apartment upstairs. The board of directors claims that any harm was actually caused by the damaged unit's own leaking bathroom appliances. If the neighbor, the unit owner, and the building all have the same insurer, then the cause of the damage does not play an important role for the insurance company. It has to cover the damage no matter where the fault lies. Of course, you cannot control which insurer your neighbors select. However, while the single insurer idea is good on general principles, follow it only when the cooperative or condominium is using a reputable and financially sound insurance company.

OBTAIN REFERENCES

As you've done with your attorney and other resources throughout the home buying process, do not underestimate the importance of educated insurance shopping. You should seek out a number of references and ask as many questions as possible. Satisfied customers who have had claims are usually the best sources from whom to ask recommendations. Determine as well whether your source ever filed a claim. When interviewing potential insurers, ask plenty of questions about pricing, the types of coverage, and the best and worst things about their particular insurance policies.

WHAT YOU SHOULD KNOW BEFORE MAKING A CLAIM

Although they rarely warn you ahead of time, insurance companies may drop you from coverage or raise your policy rate significantly when the one-year contract expires. Such a withdrawal of coverage is legally permissible and may affect your ability to obtain coverage from another insurer. Since insurance companies expect an average of one claim every seven years, a homeowner may want to resist filing a claim until it is significant and costly. Another rarely mentioned fact is that insurance companies keep a shared database on customers' insurance claims history. Customers may obtain a copy of their own database report once every twelve months.

MY STORY: THE IMPORTANCE OF
HOMEOWNER'S INSURANCE

New York City crunches millions of people into less than 304 square miles. For that reason, even its richest residents have neighbors immediately below, above, in front, behind, and to the right and left of their homes. Many times, this proximity causes neighborly interferences, most commonly from noises or leaks. The more valuable the apartment, the more likely it is to house unique and irreplaceable items and so engender panic in the event of fire or flood due to the incredible replacement costs of those things that are even capable of being replaced.

Recently, my law firm received a call to duty from one of the most impressive persons I have ever encountered. When we met, she gleamed with joy, spoke in one of the most charming voices I'd ever heard, seemed knowledgeable on almost every subject, and stimulated my intellectual curiosity within minutes. One of this woman's favorite hobbies happened to be collecting ancient maps and artifacts from all over the world. By the time she retained my firm, she had suffered four leaks from the apartment upstairs in four different places. As a result, many of these treasures had been greatly damaged or completely ruined.

After months of my client being ignored by her upstairs neighbor, she retained us to motivate him—via a lawsuit—to take measures to prevent future leaks. Ancillary to the prevention measures, she asked us to file a claim with her homeowner's insurance company to pay for the repair or replacement of the damaged items. I felt confident in the case when I saw, upon investigation, the insurance company with whom she had insured her possessions. After working with so many companies over the course of so many cases, I have acquired a sense of who pays and who fights—and this company seemed generally to pay and rarely to deny a claim for damages. In this situation, they followed through with their promise and paid every dime for which we were able to provide reasonable documentation.

It was not only to my client's credit that she had selected a reputable insurance company; she also had the proper provision to cover her property for damage due to leaks. Such a clause is not necessarily typical with insurance policies—the most common policy excludes certain perils, including flood, underground water, and seepage, although these can be covered by endorsement to the policy. Due to this provision, the homeowner's insurance company completely fulfilled its function and

(continued)

(*continued*)

made our law firm look like heroes. Furthermore, they were extremely helpful and cooperative in making sure that my client's apartment was put back into shape and the damaged possessions repaired, replaced, or—if that was impossible—the claims were paid on them.

As far as preventing future leaks, after a lot of arguing in and out of court for almost two years, we were able to settle the case and convince the upstairs neighbors to remove the illegal bathroom causing the major leaks. We established that for as long as they owned the apartment, they would place drip pans underneath the radiator and toilet which had caused the other leaks.

CHAPTER SUMMARY AND INSIDER TIPS

- Do not underestimate the importance of educated insurance shopping. Seek out referrals from satisfied customers who have tried and tested their insurance providers to find the best policy for you. When interviewing potential insurers, ask them as many questions as possible about pricing, different types of coverage, and the best and worst things about their insurance policies. Determine as well whether your source has actually filed a claim with the insurance company.

- Many insurance companies also cover the loss of your property when it is stolen or lost in a place other than your home; some standard policies even cover luggage lost overseas. You should check with the agent to find out exactly what coverage is included in each company's standard policy.

- You must be prepared to prove the value of personal property and belongings destroyed if an incident or disaster occurs. Make sure you keep a proper inventory listing all of the personal items in your home; you should also list the inventory in an e-mail and send it to yourself and another person periodically.

- It is worth supplementing your inventory list with a video recording or pictures of the insured property. Make sure that you also preserve receipts and credit card statements, and that you constantly update your inventory to include new purchases.

- Remember that insurance companies expect an average of one claim every seven years, so you may want to resist filing a claim until it is significant and costly. Insurance companies may drop you from coverage or raise your policy rate considerably after the one-year contract expires. Also, because insurance companies keep a shared database on customers' claims history, a history of frequent claims may destroy your chances of obtaining insurance through another company.

- Many people erroneously believe that their policy will insure the value of the house including any appreciation. But coverage is limited to the amount of the policy, unless you purchase additional protections. You should inform your insurance company in writing of any major improvements to your home, and ask them to add coverage to the policy accordingly.

- Do not assume that every possible type of disaster or damage is covered by the policy. Some standard policies cover terrorist attacks but not acts of war. It is not common for a policy to cover nuclear attacks or spills, and many basic standard policies exclude flood, earthquake, and lead paint casualties, although you can usually purchase these policies at extra cost.

- State and federal governments may occasionally step in to help when the insurance companies bow out. You can purchase these additional insurances through your insurance agent, and you should ask your agent what kinds of insurance your state offers.

- For cooperative and condominium purchases, you may want to use the same insurance company that insures the building to insure your individual unit and its contents, provided that the cooperative or condominium is using a reputable and financially sound firm. Using the same insurer could prove beneficial when making a claim, since it would eliminate the debate as to which insurance company should cover each particular issue.

Chapter 17 The Purchase of Title Insurance

Though owning real estate is one of the most valuable freedoms granted by our nation, it does come with some risk. Title insurance can serve to eliminate those risks and the losses associated with events that may have occurred long before the buyer bought the property. It is therefore strongly recommended that any purchaser of real property obtain a suitable form of title insurance.

WHAT IS TITLE INSURANCE?

The primary function of title insurance is to protect owners in the event of an actual defect in the chain of ownership and against hidden hazards that may threaten an owner's financial investment in the property. Title insurance typically covers everything contained within your property's survey, which is a detailed map that encompasses your property's boundaries and landmarks.

If you are obtaining a mortgage, it should be noted that your lender will require you to purchase a title insurance Loan Policy for itself in addition to your Owner's Policy of title insurance. The differences between these two policies are explained in the next two sections.

The Owner's Policy

An Owner's Policy of title insurance is a contractual obligation whereby the title company agrees under the terms of a contract called a *title policy* to indemnify an owner due to the loss of an ownership interest in the property. This kind of policy is purchased at closing for a one-time fee, and it reimburses the property owner if there is a legal barrier to occupancy, use, or resale of the insured property or a portion of it.

An Owner's Policy continues for as long as the owner owns the property. Keep in mind that payment made due to a loss or defect in the ownership of the property is valued at the date you purchased the property——not the current fair market value of the property. However, you can pay a higher premium for reimbursement of value at the time of loss.

The Loan Policy

This title insurance policy insures that the lender is receiving a valid lien on the property. Loan Policies also cover any defects in the loan, such as mortgage fraud or a forgery where an imposter pretending to be the seller collects loan proceeds.

Although the lender is the party who receives the protection here, the purchaser is usually required to pay for it. However, while the Owner's Policy should continue for as long as you own the property, the title insurance Loan Policy's relevancy to the purchaser terminates upon the proper transfer of funds to the borrower.

WHO PAYS FOR TITLE INSURANCE?

Typically, the purchaser pays for all title insurance policies. However, you should find out what the custom is within your locality, since the party that pays for the Owner's Policy can vary between states and even between counties within the same state. For instance, while the buyer would customarily pay for their own Owner's Policy in New York, New Jersey, Pennsylvania, and other East Coast states, it is the seller that would normally purchase the Owner's Policy for the buyer in Colorado, Illinois, certain counties in California, and other states. Additionally, in some areas such as Birmingham, Alabama, it is customary for the buyer and the seller to split the cost of the Owner's Policy.

WHY AN OWNER'S POLICY SHOULD ALWAYS BE PURCHASED

Although I firmly believe that all attorneys should *insist* that their clients acquire a title insurance policy—and most lenders will not issue a mortgage without a Loan Policy—such a purchase is not required by law. Countless issues may arise that threaten an owner's property interest, thereby creating the need for title insurance. If the insured party has any damages or difficulty selling the house as a result of these situations, the title company will pay for all of the legal fees and costs to defend the action and reimburse the insured party with the value of the property as of the date of purchase, if a loss occurs.

Developed in the United States and sold freely in every state except Iowa (which controls and regulates its sale), title insurance provides owners with confidence and security. Homeowners know they can safely act as if they are the true owners of the property purchased, even if later events try to prove otherwise. Without title insurance, real estate purchase and sale would be much riskier, and in turn, far less valuable.

THE FUNCTION OF A TITLE INSURANCE COMPANY

You can order your title insurance from a title company once all parties have signed the contract of sale. The title company then searches all records involving the property and traces its ownership history, usually for at least 30 years. After searching and examining the property, the title company then provides you with a written title report. In order to get insurable title, you must resolve any defects in the chain of title to the property, which is also subject to change up to the completion of the closing. Investigation of title defects includes unpaid judgments against the seller, unpaid taxes, liens on the property from unpaid contractors, unsatisfied mortgages, restrictions limiting the use of the land, and any other encroachments to the property.

In a number of states, a settlement agent or title company, instead of an attorney, works with the buyer and the seller to transfer the home. This agent takes all the necessary steps to research the home's title history and correct any defects. This includes checking for any liens, paying off old mortgages, collecting government taxes, and filing paperwork with the proper parties at court.

Unfortunately title insurance is not generally purchased in some areas; instead buyers hire attorneys to do an abstract that researches a home's history of ownership for at least 30 years. These attorney abstracts do not provide the buyer with any insurance. However, the search serves to better inform the buyer that the seller has the power to transfer the home to them.

THE COST OF TITLE INSURANCE

Title insurance rates vary between states. In several, including Florida and Texas, the State Department of Insurance decides the premiums. In many others, such as New York and New Jersey, state law determines that title insurance rates be regulated by rating bureaus. For this reason, the costs of title insurance between companies tend to be in a similar range to one another. However, in other parts of the country, including Georgia, Illinois, and Massachusetts, the cost of title insurance is not state regulated. Therefore, you may find greater rate variation in these areas.

To give you a general idea, according to the American Land Title Association, a title insurance policy tends to cost about 1/2 to 1 percent of the property's purchase price, and the average price of a title insurance policy is $700 nationwide (American Land Title Association). Your attorney can advise you about the customs of your locality.

EXAMPLES OF WHEN TITLE INSURANCE BECOMES IMPORTANT

One typical area in which title insurance becomes important involves the recording office. This is the place where documents are recorded which let the world know that a property has a new owner. These offices occasionally make errors while handling the documents. In some cases, the fault does not lie with the recording office but with the owners or their agents who have failed to record deeds.

Title insurance also protects against losses that result from fraudulent or forged transfer documents, and thus it prevents someone else from taking the property. We are now in the midst of a title fraud epidemic. Fraudulent claims greatly increase the overall number of title claims during times of decreased lending restrictions. Many of these types of claims occur because an imposter who is pretending to be the owner of record obtains a mortgage for a property using fake identification or a forged power of attorney. With this kind of crime becoming more rampant, the need for title insurance has become more important than ever before.

Consider this true story illustrating the importance of title insurance. There was a seller who sold the same property to two different people 24 hours apart and collected the purchase price from both. Because both buyers had purchased title insurance, the title companies were left to figure out who actually got to keep the property and who had to be reimbursed for the theft. The title companies also had to cover the legal expenses entailed.

One reason commonly given for purchasing title insurance is: "What happens if some Native American tribe claims the land your house sits on actually belongs to them under one of the many treaties the federal government has disobeyed?" One such New York case involved 3,100 square miles of land stretching from the St. Lawrence Seaway to the Pennsylvania border. A particular Native American tribe claimed that the land was illegally acquired and violated several agreements and treaties. The title companies provided a defense for the existing homeowners on the stretch of land in question. If the tribe had prevailed, the title company would have had to pay to those policyholders the price of the land as it was valued at the respective dates of purchase.

In most states, *adverse possession* occurs when one landowner claims another's property because of having occupied it for 10 years or more. One dispute involved five feet of property that had two small dwellings adjoined at the backyards. Though one individual claimed ownership by adverse possession, the owner of record sued upon realizing that the abutting owner had built a fence some five feet inside the border. The other owner sued back, claiming ownership of the land as a result of satisfying the technical requirements of adverse possession. Because the property had changed hands during the adverse possession period, the title company had to step in to cover both the legal fees and any resulting loss from the lawsuit.

In the above cases, the insured would ask the title company to defend the owner's rights in the lawsuit, relieving the insured of having to pay legal fees. In addition, the insured may be able to recoup any financial losses from any loss of property.

TITLE INSURANCE AND PURCHASING A COOPERATIVE APARTMENT

Although purchasers of cooperative apartments may obtain title insurance for their units, most buyers do not obtain insurable title. In a cooperative, the underlying building or the cooperative corporation should have its own title insurance for the property. Buyers should then remind their attorneys to review the building's title policy to ensure that proper coverage has been issued by a reputable title company. However, it is not common practice for an attorney to actually inspect these title policies. While most banks will not permit a buyer to receive monies for a loan without title insurance, title insurance is not customarily purchased when the closing involves a cooperative apartment. Instead, a lien search—which does not convey any form of insurance—is normally ordered. Lien searches investigate the property and unit to determine whether any encumbrances such as judgments, liens, or unpaid taxes and claims, burden the home.

THE ABSTRACT

In a few parts of the country, including some areas of upstate New York, a buyer's attorney typically orders an abstract instead of title insurance when a purchase does not involve a bank loan. This document provides a history of title to the property with copies of all relevant documents and is prepared by an abstracter, who runs a history of the property for at least 30 years. He or she checks public records to uncover ownership information and any liens or encumbrances.

The buyer's attorney then reads the abstract and checks public records to bring it up to date. The attorney will then certify to the buyer that the title is good.

Keep in mind that since abstracts do not provide actual title insurance, a mistake in this document may put the buyer's investment and possession of the home in jeopardy. Abstracts fail to address other important issues that title insurance covers, such as boundary disputes, adverse possession, identity theft, forgeries, and other forms of fraud. All these are outside the scope of a title abstract.

MY STORY: THE IMPORTANCE OF TITLE INSURANCE

I got the panicked call at about 7 PM one evening from Earl, a friend and fellow real estate attorney.

"Adam, I really, really screwed up, man," he said, sounding out of breath. "I need help big time. I'm desperate."

Earl went on to explain that he represented a buyer named Pura Rivas who was purchasing a two-family home from a seller named Alan. The terms of the deal were fairly unorthodox, since Alan had inherited the home after his father's death. Because he had alcohol and money problems, the terms dictated that Pura give Alan a certain amount of cash at the time of signing, in addition to paying for Alan's beer and food expenses for an additional six months through an account they opened together at the corner grocery. After six months, Pura would make another payment to Alan, and would then become the legal owner of the home. However, the parties agreed that Alan would live rent-free in one of the building's apartments for the rest of his life. The signed deed would not be recorded with the county clerk's office, but was instead to remain in Earl's safe deposit box until the six months had passed and Pura made the final payment.

"However," Earl continued, "I just found out that Alan had already sold the building to someone else before he sold it to Pura. This previous purchaser knows about the deal with Pura and may have already had his closing. He may have even sold the home again, himself! What do I do?"

I paused for a moment—and then I began delivering commands like I was avoiding rapid gun fire. "Even though she hasn't paid for and does not have title insurance, get your title company on line at the clerk's office at 7AM tomorrow morning. It opens at 9 AM, so you should be

(*continued*)

(*continued*)

first. Remember that it usually takes two weeks for the office to record a deed, but if you hand deliver your deed in person and have it recorded while you wait, we may be able to beat the second buyer to the recording finish line. As you know, under the law, the first to record without notice of a prior sale becomes the rightful owner."

I suggested we also visit the disputed property to learn more information about this alleged sale. I knew that if we were going to obtain any evidence about the fraud, we needed to do it now and not wait until the second buyer lawyered up.

Earl picked me up the next evening and we headed to the property. When we got out of the car, the second buyer—an imposing man named Dewey—approached us and asked what we wanted. Dewey announced that he was the rightful owner of the property, holding papers in his hand. While I don't remember what was said next, I do remember Dewey taking a shot at my face with his fist. It certainly wasn't the hardest punch I had ever taken, but I hit the ground anyway, hoping that the spectacle would cause him to be reasonable, or at least result in his arrest. This did not work.

But the plan of getting in line first at the recording office did. Two days later, the computer printout indicated that Pura's deed recorded the purchase of her home 24 hours before Dewey. Knowing the law, we knew that we now had a decent chance of winning possession of the home. Within a few weeks, I was in court representing Pura. Because Dewey purchased title insurance, he was provided with a free attorney, and a very good one.

From that point on, things only got worse. The State Supreme Court judge ruled in favor of Dewey, stating that although we had recorded the deed first, Dewey conducted the first closing, and we had known about the transaction. We of course appealed immediately. My client's life savings and dream of homeownership and Earl's bank account were on the line—as a result of his failure to advise his client to record the deed in a timely manner. No title insurance company was going to act as savior and pick up the bill for Pura.

A few months later we received the decision from the Appellate Division in the mail. We had won. The Appellate Division decided that since Pura recorded her deed one day before Dewey, the fact that Dewey closed on the property before Pura was irrelevant—and Pura was the rightful property owner.

Pura still owns her home and has paying tenants to provide extra income. I assisted her in evicting Alan from the property, as well as his friends that occupied the other apartment in the building. Pura and I still keep in touch and she recently reported that her daughter, Stephanie, will be attending John Jay Criminal College next year in hopes of becoming a lawyer. As for Earl, he joined his wife and has created a successful real estate practice. He has never failed to order title insurance again. In fact, Earl and Pura may be the best advocates for title insurance in the world as a result of their experience with this potential nightmare. As for me, the title company that hired an attorney for my adversary wound up asking me to represent them in a different case, and they still continue to be one of my favorite clients to this day.

While this story ends happily for Pura, the absence of title insurance could have turned it into an infamous buyer's horror story if we had recorded the deed just one day later. Pura was extraordinarily lucky. I cannot stress enough how essential the purchase of title insurance is for all future homebuyers. Unfortunately, in the end, Dewey may have also come out a winner; if the title company did not prove his fraud, they would have been required to pay him the value of the property.

CHAPTER SUMMARY AND INSIDER TIPS

- When obtaining a mortgage, your lender will require you to purchase a title insurance Loan Policy. Even though it is not required by law, you should always purchase an Owner's Policy of Title Insurance. Both foreseeable and unforeseeable issues may crop up and threaten an owner's property interest, thus creating the need for title insurance.
- Your attorney, settlement agent, or real estate professional can order title insurance once all parties have signed the contract of sale.
- You should find out what the custom is within your locality regarding which party pays for title insurance, since this can vary from one place to another. Buyers customarily pay for the Owner's Policy in many locations, including New York, New Jersey, Pennsylvania, and other East Coast states. However, sellers normally purchase the Owner's Policy for buyers in other states, including Colorado, Illinois, and parts of California. In other areas still, it is customary for buyers and sellers to split the cost. Speak to local real estate professionals to learn the standard procedure in the area where you wish to purchase.
- Bear in mind that paying a higher premium will allow you to purchase title insurance for the property at market value upon a loss. Otherwise,

(continued)

(*continued*)

any payment you receive from your title insurance company for this loss will only be for the value as it was at the date you purchased the property—not the current fair market value of the property.

- Unfortunately, in some localities and under certain circumstances, title insurance is not customary; instead, attorneys order an abstract that researches a home's ownership history for at least the previous 30 years. The abstract checks public records to uncover ownership information and to reveal whether there are any liens or encumbrances on the property. However, abstracts do not provide the buyer with any title insurance. So, if homebuyers are able to purchase title insurance, it is strongly recommended that they do this instead of only ordering an abstract.

- In a cooperative, the underlying building or the cooperative corporation should have its own title insurance policy for the property. Most buyers of a cooperative apartment do not purchase an Owner's Policy. Instead, they typically order a lien search, which investigates the property and unit to determine whether there are any encumbrances.

Chapter 18 Closing Cost Guide

Determining the Complete Cost of Selling or Purchasing a Property

Purchasing a home is the single largest financial investment that most people make in their lifetime. Although buyers and sellers are well aware of the concept of a property's sale price, very few individuals consider the many additional costs involved in completing the transaction.

Closing costs are the fees and expenses that a purchaser or seller incurs in the purchase or sale of real estate, whether it's a private residence, a condominium, or a cooperative apartment. These typically include financing fees, title insurance, taxes, and attorney fees. Your attorney should provide you with an estimate at the outset, so that you are properly prepared for the bottom line figures and can avoid unpleasant surprises at closing.

One buyer or seller's closing costs will vary from another's based on a variety factors, including location of the property. This chapter discusses general closing costs for the nation, in addition to referring to those in New York State as an illustrative example.

CUSTOMARY PURCHASER CLOSING COSTS

The Survey

The survey is a drawing with particular details of the boundaries of the property that you are buying. It will show the boundaries and any permanent, visible markers of the land that you are buying. Surveys are crucial in determining which land is yours, which is your neighbor's, and the location of all structures on the land.

The title insurance company typically insures you to protect your ownership interest for all of the land mentioned in the survey. Normally, your attorney or title company orders the survey, which costs between a few hundred and a thousand dollars (depending on the location and size of the property). Cooperative and condominium buyers do not order a survey if the unit is in a high-rise building; however, those that are configured as single family buildings usually do need a survey.

Title Insurance and Related Charges

A full discussion on the benefits and importance of title insurance can be found in the *The Purchase of Title Insurance,* Chapter 17. Although the purchase of title insurance for real property is customary, many cooperative unit purchasers and lenders forego such insurance as long as the cooperative building has the benefit of title insurance. To purchase a cooperative apartment, a lien search is required instead of title insurance.

The cost of the title insurance premium for a purchaser is usually regulated by the state government and based on the purchase price.

QUICK INSIDER TIP

You should check the survey against your inspection of the property. Does the survey show the swimming pool, deck, the garage, or fences? It could be a potential problem if such permanent fixtures on your land aren't included.

Lenders also require the purchaser to purchase title insurance as a condition of giving a loan. Title companies offer discounts to clients purchasing both Owners' and Loan title insurance policies, known as a *simultaneous rate*. In the case of a new construction, the title companies usually offer a bulk rate discount. According to the American Land Title Association, the average price of a title insurance policy is $700 nationwide.

For cooperative purchasers, the lien search typically costs $250. Some title companies also offer an Eagle 9® UCC Insurance Policy, which provides insurance to cover claims against the seller that may have been overlooked during the lien search.

In addition to the title insurance premium, other customary title-related charges in New York State are as follows:

1. $350 to $500 for departmental and municipal searches including Certificate of Occupancy, violations, judgment, and bankruptcy searches.

2. Recording charges for the deed, mortgage, and Unit Owner Power of Attorney (in the case of condominium). If a Power of Attorney is used at closing to execute documents (if the purchaser cannot be present), this must be recorded as well. Recording fees are estimated as follows:

   (i) In the five boroughs of New York City: The statutory charge to record any documents, such as a deed, mortgage, or Power of Attorney, is a $37 flat fee and $5 per page. If the deed or mortgage covers an additional block it is an additional $2. If the deed or mortgage covers an additional lot it is an additional $3.

   (ii) In Westchester County: The statutory charge to record a deed, mortgage, or Power of Attorney is a $50 flat fee and $5 per page.

   (iii) In Suffolk County: The statutory charge to record a deed, mortgage, or Power of Attorney is a $75 flat fee and $5 per page. If the deed or mortgage covers an additional block it is an additional $20. There is no fee for an additional lot.

   (iv) In Nassau County: The statutory charge to record a deed, mortgage, or Power of Attorney is a $55 flat fee and $5 per page. If the deed or mortgage covers an additional block it is an additional $10. There is no fee for an additional lot.

3. $75 to $150 for endorsements to Owner's and Loan Policies of title insurance.
4. Any real estate taxes due within 60 days of closing must be paid in advance for at least six months, as a lender requirement.
5. Title closer gratuity or attendance fee: $150 to $200, often a matter of the purchaser's generosity.

Attorney's Fees

For states in which attorneys are used, attorney's fees range in amount depending on the type, sale price, and location of the property. Individual attorney's rates vary greatly. For example, in upstate New York, a buyer can find a capable attorney for $500 plus charges for additional services. In New York City, real estate attorneys charge anywhere from $1,500 to many thousands of dollars depending on the purchase price, the time involved, and complexity of the deal. Some cases simply require a flat fee based on the purchase price, called a *sliding scale flat fee*. For example, one law firm charges $2,000 for a purchase price up to $1 million. If the purchase price is over a million dollars, the fee quoted becomes $500 more for each $500,000 over a million dollars. Therefore, if the purchase price were $3 million, the attorney's fee would be $3,000. There may be a supplementary fee if the closing takes place outside the county where the attorney's office is located. In the event that the closing begins and then has to be postponed for some reason, the attorney may also add an additional charge. As a general rule of thumb, you can expect higher attorney's fees in places where the property values are higher. Also, anything adding to the complexity of the deal could increase the attorney's fees.

The Engineer

A detailed discussion of the importance of hiring an engineer can be found in Chapter 13, *Using the Home Inspection to Lower the Price*. However, these fees normally range from $500 to $2,000 depending on the size and location of the property. Engineers should be hired and the inspection(s) completed prior to contract signing.

Financing Fees

Financing fees vary depending on the amount and type of loan and the lender. Although some of these fees may be collected during the application stage, the lender will always deduct those remaining from the loan proceeds. Thus, the lender will be turning over less money than the face amount of the loan to the seller at the closing. The difference is paid out of the purchaser's own funds. The estimates below may not be charged at every closing or may be in different amounts:

1. Appraisal fee: $400
2. Underwriting fees: $500*
3. Processing fees: $450*
4. Application fees: $300 (usually paid to lender when applying for the loan)
5. Lender's attorneys' fees: $750
6. Compensation to the mortgage broker: typically 1 to 3 percent depending on the type and the amount of the loan**
7. Real estate tax escrow: three- to six-month reserve
8. Hazard insurance premium: three-month reserve
9. Private Mortgage Insurance (PMI): percentage of the loan amount due if you put less than 20 percent down on the purchase or if the property does not properly appraise
10. Credit report fee and bankruptcy searches: $25 each**
11. Flood search: $25
12. UCC filing fee (for cooperatives only): $100 each

---

*Some of these fees are limited or prohibited in certain types of mortgage loan transactions.
**It is now illegal for lenders and mortgage brokers to receive a higher fee for convincing the borrower to a type of loan that is more profitable to the lender (and more expensive to the borrower). Ask your mortgage broker to detail in writing how his/her commission is determined.

Short-Term Interest

A purchaser will also pay at closing what is commonly referred to as *short term interest*. When a borrower makes a monthly mortgage payment, the interest is actually paid for the previous month. For example, when making an October 1 mortgage payment, the borrower is actually paying the interest accrued for the month of September.

If, for example, the closing is taking place on October 15, the first mortgage payment will not be due until December 1. Thus, when making the December 1 mortgage payment, the purchaser will be paying for the November interest. However, under those circumstances, the purchaser owes the lender interest for the period from October 15 through October 31. In order that this amount is not overlooked, this short-term interest is collected by the lender at the closing, calculating the interest day-by-day or per diem.

Adjustments: Fuel, Oil, and Taxes

At closing, the purchaser will reimburse the seller for any expenses they have paid in advance of closing for a period after the closing when the property will be owned and occupied by the buyers. Such expenses include common charges, or maintenance, oil, fuel (gas or propane, water) and real estate taxes. These reimbursements are commonly referred to as *adjustments* or *apportionments*. If these expenses are not paid in advance of the closing, the seller and purchaser will divide these charges according to the amount of time each had ownership of the property.

For example, let's consider the real estate tax bill. If the seller has already paid the bill in advance, then the purchaser owes the seller for the number of days that he or she benefits from that prepayment. Assume that the closing occurs on June 12 and that the seller has paid real estate taxes through July 31. Because the seller paid the taxes for 49 days when the buyer would own the home, the buyer must reimburse the seller for those days. The amount owed by the buyer to the seller for this adjustment can be found by dividing the amount of the bill by 365 days (assuming the bill was for a full year) to arrive at the per diem rate, and then taking the number of days owed (49 in this case) and multiplying this figure by the per diem charge.

Per Diem Rate:

Total bill	$2,190
Number of days the bill covers	365
Per Diem rate ($2190/365)	**$6 per day**

Total Amount Owed by Buyer to Seller:

Total bill	$2,190
Number of days the bill covers	365
Number of days seller has ownership of home and facilities	316
Number of days buyer has ownership of home and facilities	$365 - 316 = 49$
Total amount owed by buyer to seller	**$6 \times 49 = $294**

FIGURE 18.1   Calculation of Adjustment for Real Estate Taxes

Let's assume that the real estate taxes paid were $2,190. Calculation of the adjustment is shown in Figure 18.1.

In places where utilities are based on estimates rather than actual use, you can use the same method to calculate adjustments for the estimates. However, it's preferable for the parties to get a meter reading from the utility company as of the closing date. The calculation method used above also applies to maintenance/common charges for cooperatives. Oil, propane, coal, wood, and other fuels can be adjusted by measuring how much fuel the sellers are leaving behind and the purchase value of that fuel per unit.

PURCHASER CLOSING COSTS UNIQUE TO COOPERATIVES AND CONDOMINIUMS

Move In, Review, and Other Management Fees

In many cooperative and condominium buildings, buyers may be required to pay a variety of charges, deposits, and adjustments, such as the following:

- A move-in fee of approximately $250 to $500 (may be refundable).
- A managing agent document review fee, usually approximately $250. The agent charges this fee in exchange for their analysis of the *recognition agreements*—also known as an *Aztech Form*. This is a contract between the cooperative corporation, the borrower, and the lender, outlining what is expected of each party if the owner defaults on the cooperative loan.
- When the purchase has been financed, a purchaser will pay a fee of approximately $100 to the lender's attorney so that a record of the loan can be filed with the city or county.
- At closing, standard practice dictates that the purchaser of a condominium or a cooperative apartment pays the next month's maintenance or common charges.
- Recording fee for Power of Attorney for a condo.
- The Working Capital payment to the condominium (only on a Sponsor Sale).
- Elevator fee to reserve the freight elevator for a period of time.

CLOSING COST EXAMPLE: NEW YORK CUSTOMARY PURCHASER CLOSING COSTS

The Mortgage Recording Tax

For those purchasing one to three family homes and condominiums, a mortgage recording tax to New York State is owed by purchasers obtaining a mortgage. The tax rates vary depending on the amount of the mortgage, type, and location of the property.

1. New York City
   (i) If a mortgage secures a principal balance of less than $500,000, the tax is equal to $2.05 for each $100 of debt secured (and each remaining major fraction thereof); the lender pays an additional 0.25 percent.
   (ii) If a mortgage secures a principal balance of $500,000 or more, the tax is equal to $2.175 for each $100 of debt secured (and each remaining major fraction thereof); the lender pays an additional 0.25 percent. The additional amount to be paid by the lender may not be passed along to the borrower.

2. Westchester, Nassau, and Suffolk Counties
   (i) For all mortgages, the tax is equal to $1.05 for each $100 of
       debt secured (and each remaining major fraction thereof). The
       lender pays an additional 0.25 percent.

If the financing acquired is a negative amortization loan, the mortgage tax will be higher. In a negative amortization loan, the monthly
payment made is less than the interest owed and the remaining unpaid
interest is added to the money owed on the home. Such loans actually
have a higher and higher pay off amount, instead of having increas-
ingly smaller pay off amounts as the years pass. They also increase
the amount of mortgage tax due.

The Mansion Tax

For any home sold in New York State for $1 million or more, the
purchaser—not the seller—must pay 1 percent of the purchase price
to New York State. This is the reason you see many homes advertised
for $999,000.

The Peconic Bay Tax

For property purchased within the Peconic Bay Region of Long Island
(East Hampton, Riverhead, Shelter Island, Southampton, and Southold), the purchaser must pay to the Suffolk County Clerk, simulta
neous with the payment of the New York State transfer tax, additional
transfer taxes, similar to the additional taxes levied by New York City.

1. Throughout this region, there is a tax equal to 2 percent of the
   purchase price.
2. In the towns of Shelter Island, East Hampton, and Southampton,
   the first $250,000 of the purchase price on improved land (land
   that has buildings on it) is exempt from the tax and for unimproved land the first $100,000 of the purchase price is exempt
   from the tax.
3. In the towns of Riverhead and Southold, the first $150,000 of the
   purchase price on improved land is exempt from the tax and for
   unimproved land the first $75,000 of the purchase price is exempt
   from the tax.

There are other jurisdictions that also have transfer taxes, including the city of Yonkers.

Sponsor and Newly Constructed Property Purchases

In a sponsor sale or the sale of a newly constructed, converted, or rehabilitated property, New York State and, if applicable, New York City transfer taxes will be incurred. The seller generally pays these taxes. However, if the offering plan and/or contract of sale obligates the purchaser to pay these taxes, then the amount of the transfer taxes is considered, for tax purposes, to be part of the purchase price. The tax due is then calculated based on this so-called grossed-up purchase price. In other words, the purchase price and the city and state taxes are added together and then the transfer taxes owed (and the Mansion Tax) are calculated based on that total amount.

Additional fees that may be due in the purchase of new construction from a sponsor are:

1. Working capital deposit: Two months' (or more) common charges are deposited into the building's working capital fund to be used to fund the building's initial expenses.
2. Sponsor's attorney's legal fees of approximately $1500 to $2500.

CUSTOMARY SELLER CLOSING COSTS

The Broker's Fee

A real estate broker or agent's commission on the sale usually equals 6 percent of the purchase price. This fee may frequently be negotiated up or down. For example, many brokers receive 6 percent of the sales price when the commission is shared with another broker, and five percent when the commission is a straight sale in which only the listing broker participates in the transaction. When a buyer uses a real estate broker or agent's services, the fee is traditionally paid by the seller, even when the seller has not had any introduction to the buyer. Normally, the buyer's broker shares the commission with the seller's broker.

When utilizing a broker's services, buyers must protect their rights and responsibilities by obtaining a written agreement. No agreement should be signed that allows a real estate broker a commission unless the purchase or sale closes.

Other Seller Closing Expenses

Bank Fees

1. Pick-up fee: If a residential property or condominium unit is being sold and a mortgage is going to be paid off by the title company, it is common practice for the title closer to receive a pick-up fee to deliver the payoff check to the old lender and pick up the mortgage (or assignment) satisfied on behalf of the seller.
2. Payoff attorney fee: If a cooperative unit is being sold, the original stock and lease will be brought to closing by a payoff attorney, assigned by the payoff lender to the buyer or the cooperative corporation, who will charge a fee of approximately $450 for the attorney's attendance. There will also be a filing fee of approximately $100 to mark the cooperative loan as satisfied in the city or county records.

Liens and Judgments   If there are any liens or judgments outstanding against the property or seller at the time of closing, a portion of the sale proceeds may be used to pay these off. In a residential property or condominium sale, the title company will collect the money to pay off the lien holder and ensure that a *satisfaction* is recorded correctly so that the lien is properly satisfied. If a cooperative unit is being sold, the seller's attorney must secure any satisfactions or payoffs for items raised in the lien search that are required to be satisfied at closing.

Taxes Withheld for Non-United States Residents Selling Property   If a non-United States resident is selling a home at a price over $300,000, the seller is required under the Foreign Investment in Real Property Tax Act—more commonly known as *FIRPTA*—to have 10 percent of the purchase price withheld at closing. This tax ensures that foreign nationals will not evade tax liability. If, for some reason, the taxes owed by the seller equal less than this amount, the seller will be credited.

Seller Closing Costs Unique to Cooperatives and Condominiums

The Flip Tax   As an additional means of building revenue, many cooperatives and some condominiums impose a charge upon a unit's sale commonly referred to as a *flip tax*. This was initiated during the early 1980s conversion boom when tenants purchased cooperative apartments at a deep discount and then immediately re-sold them at market prices—or *flipped* them. This is a fee and not a tax; it's collected by the cooperative corporation, a private entity, and not the government. If you see it on a bill, it is probably identified as *transfer fee*.

Traditionally, the flip tax was only found in cooperatives. However, there is no legal bar to a condominium enacting one, so long as its by-laws specifically grant the condominium the right to do so.

The seller typically pays the flip tax—which tends to be based on a percentage of the unit's sale price—at closing. The building uses the funds generated to help raise capital for major maintenance and repairs to the common areas, especially the very expensive brick repairs so commonly needed nowadays. Since the purchaser is not really buying the apartment but instead the shares of stock allocated to that apartment in the cooperative corporation, the amount of the flip tax may also be based on the number of those shares. Some cooperatives have imposed a flip tax based upon a percentage of the seller's profit.

In some transactions, the buyer and seller negotiate the sharing of the payment of the flip tax. When dealing with flip taxes, your real estate attorney should review the corporate documents, including the proprietary lease or declaration and bylaws, to determine whether the condominium or cooperative corporation is legally required to charge a flip tax. Unless specifically set forth in these documents, the seller and buyer are not required to pay this particular expense.

Move-Out, Lost Stock and/or Lease, and Satisfaction of Mortgage Fees   In many cooperative and condominium buildings, sellers have additional expenses:

- A move-out fee of approximately $250 to $1000 (part or all of which may be refundable) to ensure compensation to the building in the event there is damage when moving out of the unit.

- A filing fee to remove the cooperative loan from the city or county records. This fee can typically range from $75 to $100. The document used to file that loan on the government records is called a *UCC-1*. The document used to remove this from the records is called a *UCC-3*. In both of these documents *UCC* stands for *Uniform Commercial Code*.

- Sellers who either bought their apartment for cash (bank check) or paid off the loans used to purchase the apartment should have the original stock certificate and lease kept in a safe place. If either the original stock certificate and/or proprietary lease cannot be located, the managing agent will charge a fee of approximately $500 to $1,000 to prepare a Lost Document Affidavit. The cooperative may also require a bond, which is a kind of insurance policy that the originals will never show up in the wrong hands. The premiums one has to pay for such a bond can be very expensive.

Closing Cost Example: New York Customary Seller Closing Costs

The Transfer Tax   When selling any type of real estate located in New York State, you're required to pay a tax in the amount of $4 per $1,000 of the purchase price, or 0.4 percent. For example, if the purchase price is $500,000, divide the purchase price by 1,000 and multiply by 4. ($500,000 ÷ 1,000 = $500. $500 × 4 = $2,000). So, the state transfer tax on a sale price of $500,000 would be $2,000.

Additional Transfer Taxes for New York City Residents   The sale of a New York City property requires the payment of an additional tax. When a property is sold for $500,000 or less in New York City, the seller must pay New York City a transfer tax of 1 percent of the purchase price. For sale prices above $500,000, the seller must pay New York City a transfer tax of 1.425 percent of the purchase price. This is in addition to the state transfer taxes.

The Details   In order to pay these taxes and comply with the state and city law, you must file completed forms and payments with the County Clerk or City Register in New York City where the property is located no later than the 15th day after the transaction has closed. In almost all sales where a title company is involved, the title company will pay these taxes along with the deed and transfer tax documentation and require that it be reimbursed in advance at the closing. For cooperative apartment sales that do not involve a title company, the seller's attorney collects the completed forms and payments and submits them to the City Register's Office for filing. As a practical matter, these taxes are typically paid out of the down payment being held in escrow by the seller's attorney. Although they are a real expense, they only show up as the seller is walking away from the closing table with less money.

The Property Condition Disclosure Act of New York   Under the Real Property Condition Disclosure Act, a seller is required to list all of the problems associated with the home. A seller who does not provide the disclosure form must give the buyer a $500 credit at closing. Sellers who choose to list all of the problems associated with the home then become liable for any necessary repairs they may forget to list. The Property Condition Disclosure Act does not apply to condominiums or cooperatives.

The disclosure statement provides pertinent information about the property, including facts about its location, condition, age, components, and any known issues that exist. Generally speaking, the seller is better off paying the $500 credit to the buyer at closing instead of risking future lawsuits concerning the home's sale. Many buyers are all too happy to have the $500 in their pockets and worry about fixing their own homes should the need arise. If buyers did a good job with their pre-closing inspections, the $500 is almost like a house warming gift.

Taxes Due for New York Properties Sold by Out-of-State Residents   As of September 2003, New York State requires non-resident individuals, estates, and trusts to pay an estimated personal income tax on the gain, if any, from the sale or transfer of property located within New York State. When real property is sold, form IT-2663 is filed, and when a cooperative unit is sold, form IT-2664 is filed.

The estimated tax to be paid and the form to be completed must be submitted at the time that the deed is presented to be recorded right after the real property is sold. If the property being sold or transferred is a private residence or a condominium, the representative of the title insurance company will receive the payment along with completed form IT-2663 and will submit them to the New York State Department of Taxation and Finance. If the property being sold or transferred is a cooperative apartment, the seller's attorney will be responsible for submitting the completed form IT-2664 and the corresponding payment to the New York State Department of Taxation promptly following the closing.

A seller who formerly lived in another state will not be required to pay the estimated tax if the property being sold or transferred qualifies as the principal residence of the transferor/seller within the meaning of the Internal Revenue Code.

Also, under Section 1031 of the federal tax code, if the property is an investment property, the seller may be able to exchange the property for another like-kind investment property within six months of closing in order to defer the capital gains taxes on the sale.

Examples of Closing Costs: New York

New York Residential Purchase Estimated Closing Costs For two examples of closing costs for New York residential purchases at different sales prices, see Figures 18.2 and 18.3.

New York Condominium Purchase Estimated Closing Costs For two examples of closing costs for New York condominiums at different prices, see Figures 18.4 and 18.5.

New York Cooperative Purchase Estimated Closing Costs For two examples of closing costs for New York cooperatives at different prices, see Figures 18.6 and 18.7.

Closing Thoughts on Closing Costs

It is important to realize that the purchase price of the property is only the beginning of the expenses associated with the transaction. For buyers trying to figure out what property they can afford, it is important to know prior to signing a contract of sale what you can expect

Based upon:

Sales Price:	**$ 370,000.00**
Mortgage Amount:	**$ 259,000.00 (70% LTV)**
Lender's Attorney Closing Fee	$ 800.00
Estimated Loan Charges/Escrows	$ 2,100.00
Estimated Purchaser's Attorney Fees	$ 2,000.00
Lender's Title Insurance Policy	$ 370.00
Owner's Title Insurance Policy	$ 1,660.00
Title Searches, Recording Fees & Related Charges	$ 1,200.00
Mortgage Recording Tax	$ 4,632.00
Title Closer Fee	$ 150.00
Survey Fee	$ 750.00
Escrow and Adjustments for Maintenance, Water, Taxes (at closing)	TBD
Total Estimated Closing Charges	**$ 13,662.00**
Details of Purchase	
Purchase Price of Property	$ 370,000.00
Add: Closing Costs	$ 13,662.00
Total of Above Items	$ 383,662.00
Less: Mortgage Amount	–$ 259,000.00
Deposits on Contract	–$ 37,000.00
Cash Required for Closing	**–$ 87,662.00**

FIGURE 18.2 Estimated Closing Costs for New York Residential Purchase at Sales Price $370,000

Based upon:

Sales Price:	$ 2,860,000.00
Mortgage Amount:	$ 2,000,000.00
	(69% of sales price)

Lender's Attorney Closing Fee	$ 750.00
Estimated Loan Charges/Escrows	$ 12,000.00
Estimated Purchaser's Attorney Fees	$ 2,000.00
Lender's Title Insurance Policy	$ 2,300.00
Owner's Title Insurance Policy	$ 11,315.00
Title Searches, Recording Fees & Related Charges	$ 1,000.00
Mortgage Recording Tax	$ 38,470.00
NYS Transfer Tax	$ 0.00
NYC Transfer Tax	$ 0.00
Mansion Tax	$ 28,600.00
Total Estimated Closing Charges	**$ 96,435.00**

Details of Purchase

Purchase Price of Property	$ 2,860,000.00
Add: Closing Costs	$ 96,435.00
Total of Above Items	$ 2,956,435.00
Less: Mortgage Amount	−$ 2,000,000.00
Deposits on Contract	−$ 286,000.00
Seller Concession	−$ 100,000.00
Cash Required for Closing	**$ 570,435.00**

FIGURE 18.3   Estimated Closing Costs for New York Residential Purchase at Sales Price $2,860,000

Based upon:

Sales Price:	**$ 220,000.00**
Mortgage Amount:	**$ 165,000.00**
	(75% of sales price)

Lender's Attorney Closing Fee	$ 750.00
Estimated Loan Charges/Escrows	$ 3,000.00
Estimated Purchaser's Attorney Fees	$ 1,850.00
Lender's Title Insurance Policy	$ 267.00
Owner's Title Insurance Policy	$ 1,103.00
Title Searches, Recording Fees & Related Charges	$ 1,000.00
Mortgage Recording Tax	$ 2,940.00
Adjustments for Taxes, Accrued Rent and Common Charges (at closing)	TBD
Total Estimated Closing Charges	**$ 10,910.00**

Details of Purchase

Purchase Price of Property	$ 220,000.00
Add: Closing Costs	$ 10,910.00
Total of Above Items	$ 230,910.00
Less: Mortgage Amount	−$ 165,000.00
Deposits on Contract (tenant purchaser)	−$ 22,000.00
Cash Required for Closing	**$ 43,910.00**

FIGURE 18.4   Estimated Closing Costs for New York Condominium Purchase at Sales Price $220,000

Based upon:

Sales Price:	$ 795,000.00
Loan Payoff:	$ 636,000.00
Lender's Attorney Closing Fee	$ 875.00
Estimated Commitment Fee and Loan Costs	$ 690.00
Estimated Interim Interest	$ 2,000.00
Estimated Credit Report	$ 70.00
Lien Search	$ 250.00
UCC-1 Filing Fee	$ 100.00
Courier Fees	$ 50.00
Managing Agent Fee	$ 500.00
Move-In Fee	$ 500.00
Purchaser's Attorney (excl. disbursements)	$ 2,000.00
Next Month's Maintenance and Assessment	$ 1,164.00
Maintenance Adjustment (based on closing date)	TBD
Total Estimated Closing Charges	**$ 8,199.00**

Details of Purchase	
Purchase Price of Property	$ 795,000.00
Add: Closing Costs	$ 8,199.00
Total of Above Items	$ 803,199.00
Less: Mortgage Amount	−$ 636,000.00
Deposits on Contract	−$ 79,500.00
Cash Required for Closing	**$ 87,699.00**

FIGURE 18.5   Estimated Closing Costs for New York Condominium Purchase at Sales Price $795,000

Based upon:

Sales Price:	$ 715,500.00
Mortgage Amount:	$ 465,075.00
	(65% of sales price)

Lender's Attorney Closing Fee	$ 850.00
Estimated Loan Charges/Escrows	$ 3,000.00
Estimated Purchaser's Attorney Fees	$ 2,000.00
Lender's Title Insurance Policy	$ 596.00
Owner's Title Insurance Policy	$ 2,872.00
Title Searches, Recording Fees & Related Charges	$ 1,100.00
Mortgage Recording Tax	$ 8,341.35
Common Charge and RE Tax Adjustment	TBD
Next Month's Common Charges	TBD
Total Estimated Closing Charges	**$ 18,759.35**

Details of Purchase

Purchase Price of Property	$ 715,500.00
Add: Closing Costs	$ 18,759.35
Total of Above Items	$ 734,259.35
Less: Mortgage Amount	−$ 465,075.00
Deposits on Contract (tenant purchaser)	−$ 71,550.00
Cash Required for Closing	**$ 197,634.35**

FIGURE 18.6   Estimated Closing Costs for New York Cooperative Purchase at Sales Price $ 715,500

Based upon:

Sales Price:	**$ 1,185,000.00**
Mortgage Amount:	**$ 651,750.00 (55% LTV)**

Lender's Attorney Closing Fee	$ 675.00
Estimated Commitment Fee and Loan Costs	$ 190.00
Estimated Interim Interest	$ 2,000.00
Estimated Credit Report	$ 50.00
Lien Search	$ 250.00
UCC-1 Filing Fee	$ 100.00
Courier Fees	$ 50.00
Mansion Tax	$ 11,850.00
Managing Agent Fee	$ 200.00
Move-In Fee	$ 300.00
Total Estimated Closing Charges	**$ 15,665.00**

Details of Purchase

Purchase Price of Property	$ 1,185,000.00
Add: Closing Costs	$ 15,665.00
Total of Above Items	$ 1,200,665.00
Less: Mortgage Amount	−$ 651,750.00
Deposits on Contract	−$ 118,500.00
Cash Required for Closing	**$ 430,415.00**

FIGURE 18.7   Estimated Closing Costs for New York Cooperative Purchase at Sales Price $1,185,000

to pay in closing costs. This information can help prevent unwanted, even catastrophic surprises at the closing table and ensure a smooth and seamless closing.

Conclusion

This book came from the home buying experiences of myself, my clients, and real estate experts from across the nation. May you follow the footsteps of these people to guide you toward your real estate dream, be it finding your perfect home or learning to use real estate to create wealth.

Acknowledgments

More than 50 real estate professionals, including brokers, lawyers, engineers, insurance agents, mortgage brokers, and bankers spent an incredible number of hours striving to make this book into one of the best ever written on home buying. I want to thank all of them, especially those who made this book a large part of their lives.

I first want to thank Lewis Taishoff and Alice Davidson for their insightful tips and edits, which have greatly improved the book.

Second, Dov Treiman is one of the few true geniuses that I have ever encountered. It is my good fortune to work with him as my legal partner. He belongs with the greats—Einstein, Freud, Beethoven—except his greatest expertise is in real estate law. I thank him for constantly improving my voice, improving the book's content, and working to make sure each page strives for perfection.

Last but not least, I want to thank Amanda Sam, whom I refer to as my muse. Amanda has spent the most recent year of her life primarily working on this book. She has been an incredible editor and has inspired and pushed me to make this book better and better. Her editing has sharpened my writing and has made me appear a much better writer than I deserve credit for being. She has also been my radar and test audience. If she did not understand a statement or theory, I rewrote the subject until she no longer had any questions. As Amanda attends Columbia Law School, she can start her legal career knowing that she is already a star, even before she takes her first class.

Index